"This is the best introduction to the Bible in the early church currently available. In clear and accessible prose, González surveys the Bible as a physical artifact, its uses in various settings, and the different ways it was interpreted by its earliest readers. *The Bible in the Early Church* is both conversational and dependable, hallmarks of González's scholarship over the decades. The book is ideally suited for general readers and undergraduate classrooms."

— **Peter W. Martens**
professor of early Christianity at Saint Louis University

"Finally. A book on the Bible in early Christianity that answers the important questions that everyone asks and does it in a way that everyone will want to read. This is González at his best. He cuts to the chase, anticipates our queries, leads us to the best of the primary sources, gives us enough, but not too much, and does it all in the genre of bedtime story."

— **D. Jeffrey Bingham**
professor of historical theology at
Southwestern Baptist Theological Seminary

"Reading *The Bible in the Early Church* is like being transported across time to experience Scripture the way the first believers would have encountered it. In this excellent, accessible book, Justo González allows us to see the Bible come together before our eyes from separate scrolls, to codices, to the printing press. But he doesn't stop there; he immerses us in the world of early Christians to show us what their relationship with Scripture was like in everyday practice, worship, and interpretation. This book is a wonderful introductory resource that fosters gratitude for the generations that preserved and passed down the Bible to us."

— **Karen R. Keen**
founder of the Redwood Center for Spiritual Care and Education, Garland, Texas

"Justo L. González has gifted us in *The Bible in the Early Church* with a very personal, clear, and erudite introduction to the writing, use, and transmission of the biblical text for the life of the church. He explains from a historical and faith framework the special place and function of the Bible in the worship, education, and social order of the church. He enlightens us also concerning models of interpretation used in the past to understand three crucial themes in Scripture: creation, the exodus, and the Word. Dr. González hopes that the lessons learned from this past may be transformed into new lessons for the future. This book should be a most welcome addition to introductory courses on the Bible in theological schools and universities as well as in parochial settings."

— **Alberto L. García**
professor emeritus of theology
at Concordia University Wisconsin

THE BIBLE IN
THE EARLY CHURCH

JUSTO L. GONZÁLEZ

WILLIAM B. EERDMANS PUBLISHING COMPANY
GRAND RAPIDS, MICHIGAN

Wm. B. Eerdmans Publishing Co.
4035 Park East Court SE, Grand Rapids, Michigan 49546
www.eerdmans.com

Published 2022
Printed in the United States of America

28 27 26 25 24 23   2 3 4 5 6 7

ISBN 978-0-8028-8174-8

Library of Congress Cataloging-in-Publication Data

Names: González, Justo L., author.
Title: The Bible in the early church / Justo L. González.
Description: Grand Rapids, Michigan : William B. Eerdmans
    Publishing Company, 2022. | Includes bibliographical refer-
    ences and index. | Summary: "A concise history of the Bible
    with a focus on its composition and use within the early
    church"—Provided by publisher.
Identifiers: LCCN 2021041066 | ISBN 9780802881748
Subjects: LCSH: Bible—History. | Bible—Use. | Bible—Criticism,
    interpretation, etc. | BISAC: RELIGION / Christianity /
    History | RELIGION / Christian Living / General
Classification: LCC BS445 .G65 2022 | DDC 220.95—dc23
LC record available at https://lccn.loc.gov/2021041066

Unless otherwise noted, Scripture quotations are from the New
Revised Standard Version of the Bible.

Contents

Preface

Although I do not say so explicitly in the following pages, this book is largely autobiographical. My interest in writing about how the Bible has been seen, read, interpreted, and lived in the past stems from the Bible itself having been my companion throughout the years—my companion in different stages of life and of faith. One of the cherished memories of my childhood is an always open Bible on the sideboard behind my dad's place at the table in the dining room. I also remember a few years later going to church with my family, each one of us carrying a Bible. Mine was almost as big as I was! And I remember my grandfather teaching me to read before entering school, doing so with the Bible. Therefore, I can truthfully say that the first book I ever read was the Bible. Years went by, and, now a teenager in a time of great enmity between Catholics and Protestants in my country, one of my favorite pastimes with some of my friends was to challenge a priest or nun to debate over the Bible. At other times, with much better judgment, I allowed the Bible to challenge me. More years went by, and in seminary I learned about many instruments for the study and interpretation of the Bible—languages, commentaries, and the like. Many more years have gone by, and, with the Bible again often open on the desk of my office, as it was in my childhood home, I have written a number of commentaries and other pieces on various aspects of the Bible.

Therefore, I can say that in one way or another, the Bible has always been with me. Sometimes I have followed it; sometimes I have not. Sometimes I have understood it, sometimes not. But it has always been there.

Now well into the ninth decade of my life, I write these lines about the book that has always been my companion. I have written these pages at a time of deep anxiety for all humankind. A frightening pandemic encircles the globe. Nations that were once at war now face a common enemy. Those who used to compete with one another now have to collaborate. Current events have made it clear that the Bible was always right—that, as Paul declared in Athens, God "made all nations to inhabit the whole earth" (Acts 17:26). In a word, no matter whether we like it or not, we have discovered once again that we are all related and that we are all responsible for one another.

Quite possibly when someone reads these words, the pandemic of 2020 will have passed. Perhaps its consequences will have been as catastrophic as we now fear; perhaps not. But of one thing we may be certain: generations pass, nations pass, ideologies pass, pandemics pass . . . but this Bible that has accompanied me from my childhood shall not pass.

With that certainty, just in case you may be reading these pages at a time of contagious anxiety such as the world is now living in in 2020, I leave you with the words of the Spanish poet and mystic Teresa of Avila (in a translation by E. Allison Peers):

Let nothing disturb thee;
Let nothing dismay thee:
All things pass;
God never changes.
Patience attains
All that it strives for.
He who has God
Finds he lacks nothing:
God alone suffices.

J. L. G.
Decatur, GA

Abbreviations

ANF   *The Ante-Nicene Fathers*
BAC   Biblioteca de autores cristianos
FC   Fathers of the Church
Mansi   Sacrorum conciliorum amplissima collectio
NPNF¹   *The Nicene and Post-Nicene Fathers*, Series 1
NPNF²   *The Nicene and Post-Nicene Fathers*, Series 2
PG   Patrologia Graeca, Migne
PL   Patrologia Latina, Migne

When referring to any of these series, the volume number is followed by a colon, and then the page or column number(s). For instance, *ANF* 5:200 means volume 5 of that series, page 200.

Quotations from BAC, Mansi, PG, and PL are my translations.

Introduction

The path leading from the first ancient Bibles to the one you hold today in your hands is long, complex, and providential. It includes not only the original authors but also the long history of the people of Israel and then of the church, keeping, copying, and interpreting these Scriptures that now you are able to read. In the pages that follow we will see something about the materials that were employed in the times of ancient Christianity to copy and preserve Scripture, as well as something about the formats of the Hebrew Bible and then the Christian Bible. We will also deal with the manner in which the Bible was employed in worship, the various ways in which ancient Christians interpreted the Bible of Israel (which we now call the Old Testament), and several other matters.

But there is more to that providential path. This Bible that our ancestors in the faith have bequeathed to us was also—and is still today—a source for the nourishment of faith. In times of persecution, it was in the Bible that many believers found refuge and strength. This was a reason why some of the persecutors, rather than seeking and punishing Christians at large, sought out those who had Bibles and tried to force them to give them up, in the hope that by destroying their sacred books, they would destroy the people of God. It was the Bible that inspired the great missionaries of all ages, the martyrs who suffered as witnesses to their faith, the great teachers of the church, those who created beneficent institutions throughout the world, and others of the enormous multitude from every nation, tribe, and tongue, of which we are part. This includes our grandparents who, sitting in a rocking chair, gave us wise counsel; it includes those who worshiped with us last Sunday; it includes those who lived in faith and died for faith and whose names are unknown to the world—but not to the Lord of faith!

When this Lord of faith was asked about the resurrection of the dead, he answered by recalling that God had self-identified as "the God of Abraham, the God of Isaac, and the God of Jacob," and that "he is God not of the dead, but of the living" (Mark 12:26–27). When we read the story of Abraham in Scripture, we are not reading of a dead person, of past and outdated things, but rather of one who still lives in the Lord, just as we shall someday. We do not read the Bible only to find out what happened in the past but also and above all because we know that in reading it, we are learning about our brothers and sisters in the faith, who still live in the Lord—Abraham and Sarah, Rebekah and Isaac, Moses, Aaron, Miriam, Paul, Priscilla, John, and James.

That long chain of those who live in the Lord was not broken when the last of the apostles died. By the power of the Spirit, it has continued throughout the centuries with sisters and brothers who are spiritual descendants of Abraham, Paul, and Priscilla. They too are not simply dead; they live. They too, like Abraham, like Miriam, like David, and like Paul, while living in faith, also committed serious errors. The same is true of every link in the long chain that connects us with apostolic times. It is through this flawed chain—flawed, as we also are—that we have the Bible in our hands today, copied again and again from ancient manuscripts, now translated into our language and printed to make it more accessible. Without that chain we would not have a Bible.

Therefore we too, being surrounded by such a cloud of witnesses, run the race that is set before us. As part of that race, we study, preach, and live by this Bible that our ancestors have bequeathed to us and that today we bequeath to our descendants in faith.

Those ancestors were not perfect, however, and the Bible they have left us will reflect that. This may lead us to undervalue and even despise them. But it should remind us that we too, like them, are imperfect sinners, and that we too will err both in our lives and in our understanding. Therefore, as we consider how the Bible came to us, through such imperfect people, we cannot be self-satisfied in our attempts to correct their errors; rather, we must be fully conscious of our own fallibility and sin. Perhaps, as was true of many of those ancestors in the faith, we may be incapable of seeing our errors, and this task will be up to future generations that, judging our errors under the light of the word of God, will correct them.

Since it is absolutely true that we live only thanks to the grace of God, let us also live according to that grace, being grateful to our ancestors in the faith for their great boon in leaving us the Bible, and criticizing and correcting any errors they may have committed with the same grace and love with which we hope future generations will judge us.

1

THE SHAPE OF THE BIBLE

CHAPTER 1

The Languages and Contents of the First Christian Bibles

Christianity was born within Judaism, and therefore, among other things, it appropriated the Scriptures of Israel as its own Bible. That is the origin of what we now call the Old Testament. But in the early church there were relatively few Christians who could easily read the Hebrew text of the Bible. For some time before the advent of Jesus, Hebrew had begun to decline as a spoken tongue, and was preserved mostly in the sacred writings. What the people actually spoke was Aramaic, another Semitic language that made headway among the Hebrew people beginning at the time of the Babylonian exile. By the first century CE, Jews generally spoke not Hebrew but Aramaic—although they called this latter language "Hebrew" when contrasting it with the other common language of the area, Greek. Generally, when we read in the New Testament that someone spoke in "Hebrew," or when we are offered the meaning of a "Hebrew" word, this actually refers not to the Hebrew language of the Old Testament but to Aramaic.

Since the population at large knew little Hebrew, there were also Aramaic translations of various passages and books of the Old Testament. These are called "targums," which literally means "translations." Since Aramaic was spoken not only in Palestine but also in a vast area extending eastward into Syria and Mesopotamia, Christians as well as Jews in those areas employed these Aramaic translations.

Of greater impact, though, was the language commonly spoken toward the west of Palestine: Greek. Slightly more than three centuries before the advent of Christianity, the conquests of Alexander the Great had taken Greek culture and language to a vast area that included not only Greece and its environs but also Egypt, Syria, and Palestine. When the Roman Empire conquered the eastern Mediterranean, Greek became a language spoken throughout the empire, particularly by the learned and by those engaged in long-distance commerce. In Egypt there was a large Jewish population that soon adopted Greek as its own language. This required that the Old Testament be translated into Greek. This translation was not done all at once, nor with a single understanding of the nature of translation itself. For this reason, there were some very literal translations—to the point that the actual meaning of a passage was obscured—while others sought to communicate the meaning rather than the words of the original text. To bolster the authority of this collection of translations commonly used by the Jewish people, a legend developed claiming that the translation was done by seventy-two Jewish scholars who worked independently from one another, and when they finally compared what they had done, it was found that they had all produced identical translations. The legend gave this ancient Greek translation of the Old Testament the name "Version of the Seventy," or Septuagint—a name commonly abbreviated as LXX. The list of books included in the LXX is frequently called the "Alexandrine Canon"—which, as we shall see, is more extensive that the actual Hebrew Bible.

The LXX was the Bible Christians used as they began sharing their faith with other people among whom Greek was spoken.

This is the Bible that Paul and most of the other authors of the New Testament quote as Scripture. The main exception is the Revelation of John, which seems to quote an unknown version—although it is quite possible that as he was writing, John simply translated into Greek passages that he knew by heart in either Hebrew or Aramaic. Also, the first chapters of the Gospel of Matthew quote Isaiah and the Minor Prophets in a translation that is independent of the LXX. As in the case of Revelation, it would seem that the author of this Gospel either was making use of a different translation—of which there were several—or was simply translating passages in order to quote them in Greek.

When Christianity appeared on the scene, Judaism itself had not yet decided exactly which books were sacred. All agreed on the authority of the Pentateuch and the Prophets. The book of Psalms also had great authority, since it was frequently employed in worship, particularly on certain special days and occasions. But the remainder of the canon of the Old Testament was not yet fixed. It was only late in the first century, after the temple had been destroyed, that Judaism, led by a center of biblical studies in the small Palestinian town of Jamnia, decided which books were so sacred that it was necessary to wash one's hands before reading them. (Although mention is often made of a "Council of Jamnia," it is very likely that there was no council in the sense of a gathering of people from different areas, and that what took place was simply a process whereby the Jewish scholars and leaders in that city reached a consensus on the canon late in the first century.) It is important to note that what was primarily discussed in the development of the canon was not how particular books could be employed in theological debates but what could and should be read in the synagogue—and, later, in the church as well. Naturally, the theological content of the books affected the decisions that were made. But the formation of the canon was not first of all a doctrinal matter but a question of worship.

As has often been affirmed, worship itself is a very important factor in the theological formation of those who partake in it. Here we see that worship was also an important factor in the formation of the canon.

Frequently, the list of sacred books that became the Hebrew Bible is called the "Jerusalem Canon," in contrast to the "Alexandrine Canon." The Jerusalem Canon is similar to most Protestant Bibles today, although the order of the books is slightly different:

> *The Law or Torah*: Genesis, Exodus, Leviticus, Numbers, and Deuteronomy
> *The Prophets*: the ancient prophets (Joshua, Judges, Samuel, Kings) and the later prophets (Isaiah, Jeremiah, Ezekiel, and the twelve Minor Prophets)
> *The Writings*: Psalms, Proverbs, Job, the Song of Solomon, Ruth, Lamentations, Ecclesiastes, Esther, Daniel, Ezra-Nehemiah, and Chronicles

There were several factors leading Judaism to determine the exact limits of the canon of its Scriptures. One of them was the need to develop a measure of uniformity among a population that was now dispersed throughout the world in ever-growing numbers, and soon with no homeland. Another was the conviction of some that God's revelation originally came in Hebrew, and that therefore books written in another language should not have the same authority—although the Hebrew Bible does include brief portions in Aramaic. It is also certain that one of the forces leading Judaism to determine the canon of its sacred text was the growth of Christianity. Since one of the main instruments that Christianity employed in its quest for followers was the LXX, the Hebrew canon now made it clear that several books that were part of the LXX but that were originally written in Greek—or at least were not known in Hebrew—were not legitimate Scripture. These books are commonly called "apocryphal" or "deuterocanonical." The latter name is to be preferred, since these books in fact form a "second canon" and were never generally forbidden or declared apocryphal.

All of this resulted in a difference between the Bible that Christians used, which was the LXX (see chapter 5) and which therefore included the deuterocanonical books, and the Hebrew Bible, which excluded them. There were a few Christians, but not many, who preferred the Hebrew list, or Jerusalem Canon; but in general, the church followed the Alexandrine Canon of the LXX. When late in the fourth century Jerome produced the Latin version commonly known as the Vulgate, he wished to limit his work to the Hebrew canon, but he eventually bent to church authorities and included also the deuterocanonical books. These continued being part of the Christian Bible until the Protestant Reformation, with its emphasis on translations from the original languages, provided the beginning of a movement seeking to restore the Hebrew canon. This is why today the main difference between Protestant and Catholic Bibles is that the latter include the deuterocanonical books, whereas the former do not. In brief, this means that, with some differences having to do mostly with their order, the books of the Hebrew Bible today are the same as those in most Protestant versions.

The deuterocanonical books are Tobias, Judith, 1 and 2 Maccabees, the Wisdom of Solomon, Ecclesiasticus (not to be confused with Ecclesiastes), Baruch, and several minor additions, particularly in the books of Esther and Daniel.

The book of Tobias is the story of a Jew who, having been taken as a captive to Assyria, was blinded and impoverished and yet remained faithful in his devotion to God and in works of mercy. As in the case of Job, the sufferings of Tobias are seen as tests coming from God in order to fortify and purify his faith and character.

The book of Judith is set during the reign of King Nebuchad-nezzar, who wished to be adored as a god. Nebuchadnezzar orders his general Holofernes to subject any nations that refuse to worship him, and he gives Holofernes command of a vast army to accomplish this task. According to the story, the people of Israel had recently returned from their captivity and were governed by a council of elders. When the army of Holofernes was besieging a city in northern Israel that resisted valiantly but with little hope of success, Judith, who had been a widow for slightly over three years, dressed as attractively as she could and presented herself to the enemy army, claiming she was fleeing from the Hebrews and wished to tell Holofernes how to enter the city. In a banquet with much drinking, Judith gave Holofernes to understand that she was ready to go to bed with him. Once she was in the tent alone with the general, who was weakened by drink, Judith cut off his head, put it in a sack, and left the tent, claiming she was going out to pray. She then carried the head of Holofernes to the governing elders of Israel and told them to hang it from the city wall. When they saw the hanging head of their general, the Babylonian armies fled. Through the centuries, Christian art has frequently depicted Judith holding the head of Holofernes.

The two books of Maccabees, which in truth are only one, tell what happened after the empire of Alexander the Great was dismembered. Taking advantage of tensions and disagreements between the rulers in Syria and those in Egypt, the Jews rebelled under the leadership of Mattathias and his sons. The books carry the name of one of those sons, Judas Maccabee, meaning "the hammer" or "the sledge." Although the books were originally written in Hebrew, the Hebrew Bible did not include them due to their late date, as it was decided that only books written before the time of Ezra could be considered sacred.

The Wisdom of Solomon seems to have no real connection with that famous king. It is a praise of wisdom. The first nine of its nineteen chapters are similar to Proverbs in the nature of the material they include. The second part personifies God's wisdom as a woman and lists the evils that had befallen the Hebrew people as a result of not seeking her.

Ecclesiasticus seems to date from the second century BCE and to have been written originally in Hebrew but soon translated into Greek. The Greek version attributes the work to Joshua ben Sirach, the grandfather of the translator. In its contents it is very similar to Proverbs, for most of it is a song in praise of wisdom. However, in contrast with Proverbs, Ecclesiasticus is not a fairly loose list of wise advice, but rather follows a logical order. Near the end of the book there is also a review of the great figures in the history of Israel and the role of wisdom in their accomplishments.

The book of Baruch claims to have been written by the disciple and amanuensis of Jeremiah whose name was Baruch (Jer. 32:12-16). It is fairly short, and most of its first section is actually a prayer of penance before God asking for mercy. The second part is an exhortation to wisdom, repentance, and hope. At the end there is a supposed letter of Jeremiah against idolatry.

The differences in the books of Esther and Daniel as they appear in the Jerusalem Canon versus its Alexandrine counterpart are a series of short episodes that the Alexandrine Canon inserts in these two books. Finally, as we shall see in chapter 8, the Psalms are numbered differently, although their content is the same.

At any rate, such differences regarding the canon of the Old Testament have little to do with the disagreements between Catholics and Protestants. (The main exception is a brief passage in Maccabees that has been employed to support the doctrine of purgatory.)

As to the names of the books of the Old Testament, there are some differences between the ones they have in Protestant

Bibles and those found in traditional Catholic Bibles. Most of these differences apply to the historical books. What Protestants call the two books of Samuel and the two books of Kings are the four books of Kings in traditional Catholic Bibles. What Protestants call the two books of Chronicles, older Catholic Bibles call Paralipomena, a word meaning "other things" or "the rest." The books of Ezra and Nehemiah in Protestant Bibles are often the two books of Ezra in Catholic Bibles.

This complex history explains the differences between the Alexandrine Canon, which coincides with the Roman Catholic canon, and the Jerusalem Canon, which coincides with the Protestant. Furthermore, the fluidity of early canons, both Jewish and Christian, should help readers understand how it is that the Epistle of Jude in the New Testament quotes as Scripture the book of Enoch, which is not considered canonical by Jews, Catholics, or Protestants (Jude 14–15).

CHAPTER 2

The Shaping of the New Testament

The earliest Christians had no other Bible than what today we call the Old Testament. As in the synagogues, it was this Bible that was read and explained in the gatherings of the church. There are many indications that those early Christians, Jews as they were, continued attending worship at the temple if they lived in Jerusalem; or if not, at the local synagogue. As those Jewish Christians, gathered in the synagogue every Sabbath with other Jews, heard the reading of the Scriptures of Israel, they would understand them in the light of Jesus the Messiah— the Anointed One—and they would seek to convince other Jews that this was the proper interpretation of what had recently happened in Jerusalem. After that meeting in the synagogue, once the sun had set on the seventh day of the week (Saturday), and therefore now at the beginning of the first day of the new week (Sunday), Christians would gather again to break bread in memory of the passion and resurrection of Jesus, and as a foretaste and reminder of his promised return. When they were finally expelled from the synagogues, they would continue gathering to break bread, but now they would also devote time to the reading and interpretation of the Scriptures of Israel.

While Christians were thus reading and studying the Scriptures of Israel, several factors led to the production of the books we now call the New Testament and to their being collected into a canon, or list of authoritative books. These factors were mainly three.

The first of them was the need to have books that referred more explicitly to the life and teachings of Jesus, relating them to the ancient Scriptures of Israel. These books, precisely because they dealt more directly with Christian faith, rapidly took center stage in Christian worship. Thus, when in the second century Justin described Christian worship, he listed among other things the reading of the Hebrew prophets and "the memoirs of the apostles." He says:

> And on the day called Sunday, all who live in cities or in the country gather together to one place, and the memoirs of the apostles or the writings of the prophets are read, as long as time permits; then, when the reader has ceased, the presider verbally instructs, and exhorts to the imitation of these good things. (*First Apology* 67.3-4; *ANF* 1:186)

A second factor leading to the formation of the canon of the New Testament was the importance given to communication among churches, and therefore also to the correspondence and other documents that were both a means and a result of that communication. When a highly respected leader of the church—such as Paul in his travels, John from Patmos, or Ignatius on his way to martyrdom—wrote to a particular church or person, what they wrote would soon circulate among other churches and be read in their gatherings. Writing to the Colossians, Paul tells them, "When this letter has been read among you, have it read also in the church of the Laodiceans; and see that you read also the letter from Laodicea" (Col. 4:16). John's Revelation included seven letters addressed to specific churches, but certainly John expected that the entire book would be read in each of the seven churches, and possibly elsewhere. There were also other inspiring documents that circulated among the churches and that were sometimes read in worship. Among others, one may mention the Shepherd of Hermas, which originated in Rome in the middle of the second century, and the already mentioned letters of Ignatius of Antioch. Regarding these letters and the esteem in which they were held, we have the witness of Polycarp of Smyrna, who shortly after Ignatius's martyrdom wrote to the Philippians:

> The Epistles of Ignatius written by him to us, and all the rest [of his Epistles] which we have by us, we have sent to you, as you requested. They are subjoined to this Epistle, and by them ye may be greatly profited; for they treat of faith and patience, and all things that tend to edification in our Lord. Any more certain information you may have obtained respecting both Ignatius himself, and those that were with him, have the goodness to make known to us. (*Epistle to the Philippians* 13.2; *ANF* 1:36)

Finally, a third factor leading to the formation of the New Testament was the need to determine which of the many books circulating among Christians were worthy of being read in worship and which should not be read, mostly because their teachings did not agree with those of the church at large. This need was precipitated by the canon that Marcion proposed in the mid-second century. Since Marcion was convinced that the god of the Hebrew Bible was not the same as the Christian God, and that it was only Paul who fully understood this, he rejected the Hebrew Bible, for which he substituted the Gospel of Luke and the Epistles of Paul—although deleting every reference to the

Hebrew Bible from both the Gospel and the Epistles. Besides this canon proposed by Marcion, there were many other documents in circulation—none of them as early as the Epistles of Paul or the canonical Gospels—claiming to be the true teaching of Jesus, or the acts of a particular apostle. Some of these were mere works of fiction in which the imagination of some believer created stories regarding matters such as the childhood of Jesus. But some others also had a doctrinal agenda. Some put forward the doctrines of a particular gnostic teacher. Such is the case with the Gospel of Truth by Valentinus. Others advocated for absolute celibacy and rejected marriage. This was the stance of most of the apocryphal acts attributed to various apostles, such as the Acts of Andrew and the Acts of Thomas.

In brief, it was necessary both to declare some books to be authoritative and to disavow others. This led to a long process that took centuries. From an early date, there was a general consensus regarding the present four canonical Gospels as well as the letters of Paul. There are indications that, as was to be expected, each of the Gospels was particularly well known and widely used in the region of its origin. Thus, for instance, the Gospel of Luke, probably written in Antioch or its environs, seems to have been preferred in the entire region of Syria and neighboring lands. The Gospel of Mark was particularly influential in Rome, which may be explained by the following words, written in the second century by Papias, bishop of Hierapolis, but which he attributes to an unnamed "elder":

> Mark, having become the interpreter of Peter, wrote down accurately whatsoever he remembered. It was not, however, in exact order that he related the sayings or deeds of Christ. For he neither heard the Lord nor accompanied Him. But afterwards, as I said, he accompanied Peter, who accommodated his instructions to the necessities [of his hearers], but

with no intention of giving a regular narrative of the Lord's sayings. Wherefore Mark made no mistake in thus writing some things as he remembered them. For of one thing he took especial care, not to omit anything he had heard, and not to put anything fictitious into the statements. (Fragment 7; *ANF* 1:154-55)

Likewise, the Gospel of John seems to have been written in Asia Minor, and there is no doubt that originally it circulated most widely in that area.

This inclination to rely on particular Gospels in certain areas may be seen in the experience of Irenaeus, bishop of Lyon late in the second century. Irenaeus hailed from Smyrna in Asia Minor, but he headed a church in what today is southern France, many of whose members seem to have also hailed from Asia Minor. In his extensive work *Against Heresies*, he shows he had the need to defend the authority of the Fourth Gospel, arguing that just as there are four corners of the world and four cardinal winds, there must also be four Gospels that jointly witness to the gospel of Jesus Christ (3.11.8-9). These arguments suggest that, at least in the area where Irenaeus lived, some questioned the authority of the Gospel of John.

Most of the ancient lists of the books considered Christian Scripture do not include all the now universally accepted epistles; and some do include other books, such as the Shepherd of Hermas and the First Epistle of Clement to the Corinthians. Thus, these lists represent a time when there was still fluidity as Christians sought to decide exactly which books should be part of their own Scriptures, besides those they had received from the Hebrew Bible.

One of the most ancient records we have on the formation of the canon of the New Testament is the Muratorian Canon, named after its discoverer, Jesuit scholar Ludovico Antonio

Muratori. This canon is very similar to what eventually became the canon of the New Testament, but it still omits some of the shorter epistles and includes some books that would not be part of the final canon. As to the Gospels, this document says that "although each of the Gospels does affirm different things, this makes no difference for the faith of believers, for in all of them, under the guidance of the one sovereign Spirit, the same is said regarding the birth of the Lord, his passion, resurrection, his teachings to his disciples, and his twofold coming—the first time, which has already passed, in humiliation and to be rejected, and the second, still to come, in the glory of royal power."

Despite the early general consensus regarding the main books of the New Testament, the earliest surviving list that agrees in every detail with the present canon appears in a letter that Athanasius, bishop of Alexandria, wrote in the year 367. Thus, the canon of the New Testament was the result not of an official declaration by the authorities of the church but of a long, slow process that finally led to a consensus.

There is, however, a point that should be stressed again, as in chapter 1. When we think about the formation of the canon, we typically have in mind a consideration of what books may be used as the basis for theological discussions and decisions. Obviously, this was always an important consideration, with the result that some books whose theology was questionable were soon excluded from the canon by reason both of their theological views and of their more recent date. Yet the main concern of those who shaped the canon was the matter of which books should be read in worship and serve as a foundation for preaching. This is why the Muratorian Canon, referring to the Apocalypse of Peter, says that "some among us will not allow this book to be read in church." The same may be seen in the acts of a council that gathered in Carthage in the year 397. These acts, besides listing the canonical books, also prohibited "anything else to be read in church as divine Scripture"—although the council made room for the acts of the martyrs, which could be read on the anniversary of their martyrdoms, as long as it was clear that they were not taken to be Scripture. In a word, what we often forget when we think about the canon of the New Testament is that in the long process of its formation, a determining factor was the contribution a book could make to what was said and done in worship.

Finally, before leaving the matter of the formation of the New Testament, one may wonder what reason Christians had for including in their sacred writings four books that differ in so many details as do the four canonical Gospels. Already in the ancient church, some wondered about these differences. For instance, Origen, the great Alexandrian theologian, suggested in the early third century that Jesus taught his disciples two different prayers, since the Lord's Prayer that appears in Matthew is not exactly the same as the one found in Luke.

These differences would later lead some critics of Christianity to suggest that in giving canonical status to these four Gospels, Christians were not aware of the differences among them. A very common response to this allegation is to try to soften the differences by simplistic explanations that cannot withstand even a cursory reading of the Gospels. For instance, we have sometimes been told that the reason for the differences between Jesus's genealogy in Matthew and the one in Luke is that one is telling the genealogy through Mary, and the other through Joseph. Such an explanation should prove satisfactory only to those who do not take the time to compare the names appearing in these two genealogies, for the text itself of the Gospels shows that the differences cannot be explained in this manner. Others have tried to coordinate the Gospels, joining them into a single text. Already in the second century, Tatian produced such a compilation, the *Diatessaron*—a title meaning "according to the four." For some time this harmony and summary of the four Gospels was quite popular, particularly in Syria and other Syriac-speaking areas. But eventually the canon of the New Testament was determined to include four clearly different Gospels. More recently one can find a number of "harmonies" of the Gospels that in truth make the differences quite stark by placing in parallel columns similar passages that, however, do not agree on many points.

To understand why the church decided to include in the canon four different Gospels, it is necessary to take into account the challenges that those early Christians faced. The name of Jesus the Christ and his impact on society were such that soon there were many trying to join his message and his name to their own religious tendencies and schools. This was a time when people, searching for meaning in life, were often convinced that such meaning could be found only in spiritual realities, and that everything material was an obstacle on the path to truth. This was clearly contrary to the teachings not only of Jesus but also of all the Hebrew Scriptures, where God is seen as the creator of all things, spiritual as well as material. The dominant emphasis on spiritual reality over against the material led many to deny the physical reality of Jesus, or in the best of cases to consider it unimportant. Some were convinced that one's soul could gain passage to a higher sphere by knowing certain secrets that would serve as passwords. These various views are often called "Christian Gnosticism," for there were also other gnostics whose systems did not include the name of Jesus or of Christ. Late in the second century, and during the third, this situation resulted in a series of "gospels," each of which claimed to be the only true one. In general, they included supposed teachings about Jesus in which the purpose of life, and the world in general, were diametrically opposed to the witness of the Hebrew Scriptures. In response to this multitude of gospels, each claiming to be the sole true one, the church proposed a variety from the genre—four in total. While these differed among themselves on various narratives and details, they all agreed on a number of essential points of doctrine: God is the creator of all that exists, and therefore all that exists is good; there is only one God, whose relationship to creation is one of love; this God has spoken and still speaks in the Scriptures of Israel; this God was incarnate in Jesus Christ, who by virtue of his death and resurrection is the beginning of a new and restored creation; and this new creation will come to its fruition with the return of Jesus. By claiming these four different witnesses that, however, agreed on the essentials, the church was able to refute those who claimed the single witness of a later gospel.

At the same time, by including four Gospels in its canon, the church was expressing an openness to a measure of diversity within itself. Each of these four Gospels was the favorite of some within the church. While Christians in Asia Minor might prefer the Gospel of John, some in the Judeo-Christian community preferred Matthew, and people in Syria had long employed Luke. Thus, in its very variety, the canon of the New Testament opened the way for a church that could be one even in the midst of its growing diversity.

CHAPTER 3

The Physical Appearance of
Early Christian Bibles

A s one studies the origins of various cultures throughout the world, one finds that writing has emerged independently in various areas. The ancient Egyptians, the Chinese, and the Maya each developed their own form of writing. The earliest forms of writing were simply stereotyped figures of common animals and objects that eventually were associated with the sound of the word they represented. Such methods of writing required—and still do—hundreds of symbols that one must learn to be able to read and write. It was in the ancient Near East, in what we now call the biblical lands, that the first alphabets appeared—that is, the first systems making it possible to write with a rather limited number of symbols, each representing a particular sound. It is impossible to determine precisely when such phonetic alphabets appeared. Traditionally it is said that it was the Phoenicians who invented the alphabet that stands at the root of the Hebrew as well as the Greek and Roman alphabets. With slight variations, those alphabets are still used to write in a vast number of languages, including English. Apparently in the third century BCE, the Hebrews transformed the alphabet, giving it a square shape. It is this "square alphabet" that today serves as the Hebrew alphabet and that is generally used in printed Hebrew Bibles. This does not mean that the ancient alphabet was totally abandoned. Indeed, in ancient times both were used simultaneously, so that among the Dead Sea Scrolls discovered in the twentieth century, some are written in the ancient alphabet, and some in its square counterpart.

No matter whether by means of ideographic symbols or of hieroglyphics such as the Egyptians used, or with the letters of an alphabet, many different materials were employed for writing. One of the earliest was stone, as may be seen in the many lapidary inscriptions still in existence. In ancient Mesopotamia, clay tablets were inscribed and then baked to give them permanence. Another material very often used for brief notes was simply pieces of broken pottery. Given the shape of such pieces, they were called "oysters" or "ostraka." (This is the root of the word "ostracism," for in ancient Athens it was on this material that votes were cast leading to someone's exile.) In some cases, sheets of metal were employed. This may be seen in Exodus 28:36, where instructions are given for priestly vestments: "You shall make a rosette of pure gold, and engrave on it, like the engraving of a signet, 'Holy to the Lord.'" Likewise, cloth, wood, and several other materials were used. Since they are not as permanent as stone or pieces of pottery, most writings on such materials have disappeared.

While all these other materials were used, the two most common in antiquity were papyrus and leather. Papyrus—the etymological root of our present word "paper"—is a plant that grows along the sides of rivers and in marshy areas. It abounded in Egypt, and apparently it was there that the process was invented whereby papyrus fibers were used to produce something similar to what today we call paper. The Latin writer Pliny the Elder, who lived during the first century CE, left a detailed description of the manner in which this plant was processed in order to produce a writing material that was also called "papyrus." Some points of his description are somewhat confusing and difficult to understand. But at least it is clear that a needle was used to divide the stalk of the plant into thin strips. Strips taken from the middle of the stem were best and were therefore reserved for the production of high-quality material. (There was a rather detailed system for classifying papyrus according to its quality.) These strips were soaked in water from the Nile and then placed one next to the other on a board. Then a second layer of strips was laid crosswise above the first. The sheet was then pressed and dried in the sun. Normally a sheet of papyrus would be about ten inches high, and not quite as wide. Once they were dried, the sheets were glued side-by-side to create a scroll. According to Pliny, the normal limit for a scroll was twenty sheets—although some authors speak of much longer scrolls. When a scroll was lengthy, a stick was placed at each end so that it would be easier to handle and read the scroll as it was unwrapped at one end and wrapped at the other. Naturally, smaller scrolls, commonly used for less important matters or shorter messages, did not need such support. In order to protect the scrolls themselves, they were often placed in earthen vessels, as was the case with the Dead Sea Scrolls.

Because excessively long scrolls were more fragile and difficult to handle, when a document was too extensive to fit in one scroll, it was divided into two or more. Each of these was called a *tome*, a Greek word simply meaning "cut" or "division"—as in the English words "dichotomy," "appendectomy," and "lobotomy."

When the Hebrew Bible was translated into Greek, this created new difficulties, for in Hebrew only consonants were written, whereas Greek writing included both consonants and vowels. The result was that a Hebrew text became much longer when translated into Greek. Since this made some Greek translations too long, some books that in the Hebrew original were only one scroll were divided into two in their Greek translation. Such was the case, for instance, for what we now call the two books of Samuel, which in the Hebrew canon are only one.

Although papyrus was the most common material on which to write, most ancient papyri have not survived, as humidity slowly decomposes papyrus. The extant papyri come mostly from two sources: Egypt and the ruins of Herculaneum. The latter was a city that was destroyed by the famous volcanic eruption that also destroyed Pompeii—and that killed Pliny the Elder. Among its ruins, an extensive collection of documents written in papyrus has been found, preserved by the ashes of Vesuvius. However, not a single one of these documents is either Jewish or Christian. Much more interesting are the papyri found in Egypt, where the dry climate has preserved hundreds of papyri, mostly in fragmentary form. These do include both Jewish and Christian writings. Among the latter, several are fragments of the New Testament. Even in their fragmentary form, these are of great interest, for they are the most ancient copies we have of some passages in the New Testament.

The other material that was commonly used for writing is leather. This could be cut into rectangular pieces similar to the sheets of papyrus. These were then sewn together, resulting in a scroll similar to the papyrus scrolls that have just been described, although heavier and much more voluminous. Its heft made leather less convenient than papyrus, but leather had the advantage of being more durable, and therefore it was preferred for the books to be read in Hebrew worship. Eventually the Talmud stipulated that scrolls to be read in the synagogue had to be written on leather. An excessively long leather scroll would have been heavy and unwieldy. This is one reason why the Pentateuch was divided into the five books that we now have.

A particular kind of leather was parchment, also known as "membrane." This was not tanned leather, but rather a skin—of sheep, goat, or calf—that was soaked in water with lime and then stretched, dried, and scraped on both sides until it became a very fine sheet that was then cut to the desired size. Although this procedure was known and practiced from a much earlier date, in the second century BCE the city of Pergamon, which prided itself on its library at a time when papyrus was scarce, became known for the production of these "membranes," to the point that the material came to be known as *pergamena*—from which the English "parchment" is derived. Eventually the mistaken notion arose that parchment had been invented in Pergamon. The best quality of parchment was called *vellum*—a term still used by librarians and collectors. The most ancient either complete or almost complete manuscripts of the New Testament date from the fourth and fifth centuries, and they are written on parchment. We have a reference to Christian use of parchment in 2 Timothy 4:13, where we see Paul asking Timothy to bring him "the books, and above all the parchments"—which in the original Greek is literally "the membranes."

It is important to note, however, that these most ancient extant and fairly complete manuscripts of the New Testament (Sinaiticus, Vaticanus, Alexandrinus, and Bezae) are not scrolls, but rather codices. Codices consisted of several pages bound or sewn together like a modern book. Originally, these pages were wooden tablets that were perforated on the margin and joined by a cord. This is the origin of the word "codex," which derives from the Latin *caudex*, meaning "board." At first there were only two such boards joined together, in which case the volume was called a "diptych." (The word "diptych" is important in the history of ancient Christian worship, for an official diptych was used to write the names of bishops for whom a church prayed. If a bishop erased the name of a colleague from the diptych, this was tantamount to breaking communion.) Obviously, a diptych could not be used for an extensive document. Over time, more boards were added to the codex, but the thickness of the boards themselves limited the possible size. Usually the boards in a wooden codex were covered with wax, and one wrote on them by scratching the wax, which made the boards easily reusable. Such tablets would normally be used for temporary notes rather than permanent writing. Quite possibly, when Paul or any other Christian author dictated their letters and other documents, these were originally put down on waxed tablets by an amanuensis and later transcribed into a more permanent form.

It was quite apparent that a codex, either of papyrus or of parchment, was handier than a scroll. If one wishes to find a particular passage in a scroll, it is necessary to unroll it until one gets to the desired passage, whereas in a codex, all one has to do is go to the page in question. If one is preparing for a debate and wishes to have certain passages at hand, it is a simple matter to mark the appropriate pages with threads, pieces of cloth, or any other material. A preacher could easily mark a particular passage to refer to it during a homily. All this would be much more difficult when dealing with scrolls. Furthermore, although the format of a scroll is better for preserving the central part of a document, the beginning of the document itself, which must be constantly rolled and unrolled, may be damaged quickly. For all these reasons, it was precisely at the beginning of the Christian era that the codex format began displacing the scroll—although the scroll continued being used for certain sorts of official documents, and even today it is often used for awarding diplomas in commencements. Just as scrolls were protected by being kept in earthen vessels, codices were often kept in a leather box, although few remains of these boxes still exist.

Scholars still debate what possible relationship there may have been between the rise of Christianity and the growing preference for the codex format. There is certainly a chronological coincidence between the growing popularity of codices and the expansion of Christianity. The codex was known and used already in the first century, particularly in Rome. Its traditional use was similar to that of waxed tablets: jotting down brief notes or passing reminders, and not usually for literary works. This began to change in the late first century. It was at that time that the poet Martial suggested that his poetry be copied and circulated in parchment codices. Beginning at that time, codices became ever more popular. What is remarkable and difficult to explain is that this took place more rapidly within Christian circles than among the general population. Less than 2 percent of pagan Greek texts from the second century that have survived have come to us as codices—the rest are still scrolls. But the ancient papyri of the New Testament, as well as other contemporary Christian documents, were codices. Apparently in this respect Christians moved ahead of the rest of society, for beginning in the third century the proportion of manuscripts in scroll format began to decline among the population at large, while the number of codices grew. It is not clear why Christians seem to have preferred the codex before it became more widely used. It has been suggested that a codex was cheaper than a scroll, and therefore Christians, who were mostly poor, would be better able to afford it. But this does not explain why it is that even among well-to-do Christians there seems to have been a preference for codices above scrolls. Others suggest that a codex was handier in situations of controversy, for the reasons already noted. Still other scholars believe that what actually happened is that some text or texts of great authority—perhaps the letters of Paul, or perhaps a particular Gospel—circulated at first in codex format, and the process of copying it popularized that format. In truth, none of these various theories is fully convincing. All that one can really affirm is that the use of codices became popular within Christian circles much more rapidly than in the rest of society.

No matter whether on papyrus or parchment, manuscripts were written with ink. This was made by mixing water with soot, and often adding to it gum arabic or any other substance that would make it more permanent. Pliny the Elder—the same writer who left an account of the production of papyrus—records an ancient recipe for ink. This recipe, besides soot and gum, included rosin, the lees of wine, and several other ingredients. The resultant ink was black. This is why in both classical Greek and the Koine Greek of the New Testament, the word for ink is *melan*, "black." Ink was often stored dry, and water was added when it was to be used. The most serious shortcoming of this ink was its lack of permanency, for even with the addition of gum and all the other ingredients, water could easily erase or at least blur it. Someone discovered that ink would become more permanent with the addition of an extract taken from certain tumors growing on oaks. But, unbeknown to the ancients, this product tends to destroy papyrus, and therefore some of the manuscripts that used such ink have suffered serious damage, sometimes to the point of being illegible.

Although the most ancient manuscripts did not use them, there were also inks of various colors. The most common was red, which could be produced with iron oxide. Because red ink was frequently used in headings and instructions in liturgical books, today we call such notations "rubrics"—that is, writings in red. "Purple" was a very expensive dye extracted from the ink sac of a mollusk in the eastern Mediterranean. This was sometimes used to highlight the great importance of a particular document. There is also a tradition claiming that the Jewish priest Eleazar provided the pharaoh Ptolemy II with a Hebrew Bible written in letters of gold. Even though all these various sorts of ink were in existence, the biblical manuscripts that ancient Christians used were generally codices written with black ink on papyrus or parchment.

The instrument for writing on waxed tablets was a small and pointed piece of wood or metal called a *stylus*, "column"— from which our present word "style" is derived. To apply ink on papyrus, the most common instrument was a small brush made out of the stem of a papyrus plant. This is probably what is meant by "the false pen of the scribes" in Jeremiah 8:8. Later, as parchment became more common, pens were still made out of a papyrus stem, but this was now sharpened, and a small slit was made on the tip so that it would retain ink. This instrument was called *kalamos*, a word that in Greek simply means "reed." Eventually in Latin the word *calamus*, originally meaning a reed or a piece of straw, came to mean a writing instrument. When, much later, feathers were given the same use, they too came to be known as *calami*.

All of this means that when early Christians attended worship with other Christians, they could well find there the Hebrew Scriptures, still in the form of scrolls, as well as some of the writings that we now call the New Testament, but these in codex format. A bit later, all these books would be in the form of codices. This would be true of those translated from Hebrew scrolls into Greek, as well as those originally written in Greek. Still later, there would also be Latin codices.

CHAPTER 4

Chapters and Verses

Perhaps the most notable difference between ancient Bibles and those we have today is that the text of the former was not divided into chapters and verses. This is why when the book of Acts wishes to tell us that the Ethiopian was reading Isaiah 53, rather than giving us that reference, it quotes the beginning of the passage: "Like a sheep he was led to the slaughter . . ." (Acts 8:32). Today we would simply say he was reading "Isaiah 53." But the only way the ancient author could refer to a specific passage was to quote it.

Although ancient Hebrew Bibles were not divided into chapters and verses, they did have divisions showing, for instance, where paragraphs began and ended. These divisions, which were helpful when Scripture was to be read in worship, were not numbered and therefore could not be used as references. Other divisions were added later, also with a view to helping the reading of the text in the synagogue. This was a long process, and it was not until the fifteenth century that Hebrew Bibles came to have the divisions that are still used today.

Early Christian Bibles were not divided into chapters and verses either. In the fourth century, Eusebius of Caesarea proposed dividing the Gospels into chapters; but the divisions he suggested—which were different than what we have today—although used by many, were not widely accepted as a standard for all. It is in the tenth century that we finally find a biblical manuscript divided into chapters (but not into verses). From that date on, there are many Bibles divided into chapters, although these divisions vary widely.

It was late in the Middle Ages that it became common practice to divide the biblical text first into chapters, and then into verses. This became necessary partly because of the methodology followed in university studies and discussions. Many of the academic exercises in medieval universities were debates for and against a particular proposition, known as *quaestiones disputatae*. (A disputatious approach was also used, for example, in the biblical commentaries and commentaries on the *Sentences* of Peter Lombard that all professors had to produce as they sought doctorates in theology.) These "debated questions" exercises consisted mostly in posing a question or thesis and then collecting arguments both in favor of and against it. In some cases, a few days of study were granted so that students and professors could collect and organize quotes from various authorities—including the Bible. This was not easy, for there was no such thing as a biblical concordance. In order to facilitate this sort of work, those who had Bibles or other important texts added chapter numbers to them, which would then allow them to take notes and to find a particular passage at a later time. These divisions and other markings were mostly private—aids that each scholar developed and used for his own studies and academic exercises.

Although at first scholars and students simply followed their own individual divisions of the text, the system that eventually prevailed seems to have been created by Stephen Langton, who was archbishop of Canterbury from 1207 to 1228. Soon not only other Christian scholars, but also Jewish rabbis, began dividing

Scripture following the method suggested by Langton, and by the fifteenth century this was common practice.

Dividing such chapters into verses took much longer. In this also there were various systems, which obviously made all of them less useful. The one that is used today appeared for the first time in 1551, in Greek and Latin printings of the New Testament—the Greek following the text of Erasmus, and the Latin the text of Jerome's Vulgate. Two years later a translation of the Bible into French followed the same method. In 1555 the entire Vulgate was first published with a division into chapters and verses. From that point on, most Bibles published in various languages have followed the same pattern of divisions. Much of the credit for this standardization is due to French printer Robert Estienne, who served with distinction under King Francis I of France. When Francis died, Estienne, finding himself under severe pressure from the Catholic theologians of the Sorbonne and without royal support, fled to Geneva, where he continued his fruitful work as a printer, producing not only the abovementioned Bibles but also many of Calvin's works.

The edition of the Vulgate published in 1555 also had another important characteristic that is still common today. Until that time, verse numbers appeared in the margins of the text. The Vulgate of 1555 for the first time placed such numbers at the beginning of the verses themselves.

Because today the method of division into chapters and verses is almost universal, we often do not realize its importance. It is due to such divisions that we can now have concordances and other similar aids to biblical study. It is also because of that system that, whether in speaking, writing, or preaching, we are able to refer clearly and specifically to a particular passage in the sacred text.

On the other hand, there are also cases in which these divisions may hide from us the context of the entire passage. A well-known case is 1 Corinthians 13, whose praise of love many know by heart. What we often miss is that this particular chapter is the conclusion of a long discussion about spiritual gifts, and is introduced by the words of Paul in what is now the end of chapter 12: "I will show you a still more excellent way." In this case, the division into chapters tends to hide the central point: Paul's affirmation that love is a more excellent way than any of the spiritual gifts he has been discussing and which seem to hamper loving relations among the Corinthians.

Another interesting case can be found in Revelation 12:18, where there is a variant in the Greek text such that it may be read either as "he [the dragon] took his stand on the sand" or as "I took my stand on the sand." The NRSV follows the most likely interpretation by printing the text in such a way that verse 18 is clearly joined to what follows in chapter 13, and not to what precedes in chapter 12. In brief, the meaning of this particular verse depends on whether one understands it as the conclusion of chapter 12 or the beginning of chapter 13.

Students of the Bible have long noted the possibility that these divisions, while very helpful, may also hide part of the meaning of the text. Therefore, they have repeatedly reminded us that the present division into chapters and verses is not part of the canonical text and is to be used when it is a help to understanding the text but not when it hinders such understanding. A case in point is Calvin's warning regarding Genesis 12:1: "That an absurd division of these chapters may not trouble the readers, let them connect this sentence with the last two verses of the previous chapter" (*Commentary on Genesis 12.1*).

CHAPTER 5

The Transmission of the Text through the Centuries

It was almost two millennia ago that Paul wrote his Epistle to the Galatians. Therefore, we should not be surprised that the Bibles we have today have a very different appearance than those a believer would have had, for instance, in the third century. In chapter 3 I discussed the physical appearance of the Bible in ancient times, including the materials on which the texts were written and the ink and tools that were used. Now we turn to the question of how the Bible was bequeathed from generation to generation, and how this has affected the biblical text itself.

We do not have the original of any book of the Bible—what is usually called the "autograph" manuscript. What we do have are copies of copies, all handwritten and therefore quite appropriately called "manuscripts," a term derived from two Latin words, one meaning "hand" and the other, "writing." The most ancient surviving manuscripts of parts of the Old Testament date from the second century before Christ. These are among the Dead Sea Scrolls that were discovered in the twentieth century. Until then, the oldest manuscripts of the Hebrew Bible we had were from the Middle Ages, mostly from the tenth century on.

We do have very early fragments of writings that are now part of our New Testament. There is, for instance, a fragment of the Gospel of John that apparently dates from early in the second century. But this is no more than a few words long. It is only beginning in the fourth century that we find fairly complete codices. The most important of these are the Codex Sinaiticus and the Codex Vaticanus (both from the fourth century), followed by the Codex Alexandrinus and the Codex Bezae (from the fifth). In total, there are some six thousand ancient and medieval manuscripts of the New Testament or portions of it. The oldest extensive texts we have are all in capital letters, without punctuation or separation between words. These are called "uncial manuscripts."

In the process of copying and recopying manuscripts, variants have necessarily appeared within biblical texts. The vast majority of these variants have little significance. They can easily be attributed to an inadvertent error by a copyist. Such errors are very similar to those we incur today when we copy any writing. Someone omitted a word, and a later copyist, noticing that something was missing in the manuscript, had to add what seemed the most logical, which was not always exactly the same as was in the original. In other cases, the same word or phrase appeared repeatedly in neighboring places, and without realizing it, a copyist jumped from the first of these to the second, omitting what was in between. Sometimes a copyist would find a few words on the margin and had to decide if these were mere commentary by a reader, or were actually words that an earlier copyist or reader noticed had been omitted and now placed at the margin by way of correction. Or, a copyist might have encountered what seemed to be a contradiction or difficulty in the text itself and solved it by adding a few words—or perhaps by adding a marginal note that at some later point somebody else incorporated into the text.

This latter case may be seen in 1 Corinthians 14:34–35. Some modern Bibles include a footnote explaining that in some manuscripts these two verses do not appear here, but rather after verse 40. This is what scholars call a "floating text"—that is, a text that appears in different places in various manuscripts, or in some cases does not appear at all. How is one to explain such an occurrence? Most probably what happened was that a copyist or reader, coming to this place in 1 Corinthians and noticing that Paul has just spoken about the attire of women as they prophesy, even though in 1 Timothy 2:11-12 women are forbidden even to speak, copied the words from the Epistle to Timothy on the margin of 1 Corinthians. Later, other copyists coming to this place and seeing that marginal note did not know whether or where to include it, with the result that some place it where it now stands in most Bibles, and some after verse 40.

In some cases textual variants seem to be purposeful, and may even be tendentious. For instance, as we study the book of Acts, we learn that besides the text generally considered to be original—often called the "common text" or "neutral text"—there is a "Western text." Although scholars generally agree that the common text is closer to the original and that the Western text is later, the latter seems to be fairly old, for it was already circulating in the second century. In general, the Western text simply adds details or clarifications that are interesting but that do not seem to have been part of the original text. However, some of its variants do change the meaning of the text in subtle but biased ways. For example, in the Western text, Acts 17:12 is changed so that those who are "of high standing" do not include the women, and in Acts 17:34 "a woman named Damaris" is omitted from the list of converts. Finally, while the common text usually refers to the couple that worked with Paul as "Priscilla and Aquila"— except in a case in which grammar requires the reverse order— the Western text consistently calls them "Aquila and Priscilla." Thus, as a whole, one may well say that the Western text has an antifeminist agenda.

The existence of variants large and small in the texts has given rise to a discipline that is commonly called "textual criticism" or "lower criticism." In this name, the word "criticism" does not mean a negative approach to the text, but rather a critical study of the text as it now appears. And the adjective "lower" should be understood not in a pejorative sense but simply as a way to distinguish it from what is usually called "higher criticism," which deals with matters such as the date, authorship, composition, and sources of a text as opposed to the words themselves of the text. The main goal of lower criticism is to restore the text to its exact original form, mostly by deciding among existing variants.

As a discipline, textual criticism requires the comparison of manuscripts in order to come as close as possible to the original text. This is not an easy task. It is not enough simply to compare manuscripts and decide that the majority of them must be closer to the original text. It is quite possible that a variant may exist in a large number of manuscripts but not in others. In such a case, one is tempted to say simply that the majority must be correct. But, since the manuscripts we have are copies of copies that in turn are also copies, perhaps that large number of manuscripts showing a particular variant have all been copied from a single one or from copies derived from that single manuscript. Therefore, the process of lower criticism requires a more detailed examination of manuscripts, determining their "families"—that is, groups of manuscripts that seem to have a common ancestor. If a few manuscripts independent from one another agree on a text, this carries much more weight than a larger number of agreeing manuscripts all of the same family.

Another tool often used in the task of restoring the original text is comparison with ancient translations. Among the most ancient are the already mentioned targums—translations into Aramaic that began to appear during the Babylonian exile, when Aramaic supplanted ancient Hebrew as the language commonly spoken among the Israelites. The Samaritans also had their own distinct translation of the Torah into Aramaic. As we have seen, the Septuagint (LXX) is actually a series of different translations from Hebrew into Greek that were produced in Alexandria in a process that took several generations and was not completed before the beginning of the Christian era. This translation was the Bible that most of the authors of the New Testament, as well as other Greek-speaking Christians, read and quoted. Since Syriac was the prevalent language in the Middle East, the Bible was also translated into that language late in the second century or early in the third. Finally, although Greek was generally understood by the cultured throughout the Roman Empire, Latin was still the dominant language in the western parts of the empire. This required a translation of the Bible into Latin. The Vetus Latina, or "Old Latin," Bible, of uncertain origin, was based on the Septuagint (in other words, it was a translation into Latin of a Greek text that was in turn a translation from Hebrew), and it appeared in the early centuries of the Christian era. It was superseded by the Vulgate. The Vulgate is a Latin translation of the Old Testament from Hebrew, and of the New Testament from Greek, produced by Jerome in the fourth century, and it became dominant throughout the Latin Middle Ages (see chapter 1). These translations contribute to textual criticism, for when there are variants in the original language and the ancient translations follow one of them, we know that by the time those translations were made, that particular variant of the text already existed— which may mean that it reflects the original text.

The same is true of the other main source we have for the task of textual criticism: the quotations that appear in ancient Christian writings. Once again, in this case if an ancient writer quotes a variant, that is an indication that this particular variant already existed at the time when the writer quoted it, and may well be closer to the original text.

In summary, there are a number of resources that scholars employ to try to restore the original text of Scripture to the best of their ability. Therefore, the Bible we now hold in our hands is the result, first of all, of a long manuscript tradition of faithful Jews and Christians who sought to preserve Scripture, and then of a careful analysis whose purpose is to undo any errors that the long line of copyists may have made.

Ancient Christian writers were aware of such variants in the biblical text. In the late second century Irenaeus commented on a variant he found in the passage referring to the number 666 in the book of Revelation:

> I do not know how it is that some have erred following the ordinary mode of speech, and have vitiated the middle number in the name, deducting the amount of fifty from it, so that instead of six decades they will have it that there is but one. . . . Others then received this reading without examination; some in their simplicity, and upon their own responsibility, making use of this number expressing one decade; while some, in their inexperience, have ventured to seek out a name which should contain the erroneous and spurious number. Now, as regards those who have done this in simplicity, and without evil intent, we are at liberty to assume that pardon will be granted them by God. But as for those who, for the sake of vainglory, lay it down for certain that names containing the spurious number are to be accepted, and affirm that this name, hit upon by themselves, is that of him who is to come; such persons shall not come forth without loss, because they have led into error both themselves and those who confided in them. (*Against Heresies* 5.30.1; ANF 1:558–59)

Although most often ancient scholars had a single manuscript of a biblical text, they also carried a vast correspondence among themselves and thus were occasionally able to compare manuscripts. One remarkable undertaking was tackled by Origen, the great Alexandrian scholar who lived late in the second century and early in the third. Origen developed a vast system for comparing biblical texts and translations. His *Hexapla* was a text of the Old Testament in six parallel columns, hence its name. The first of these was the Hebrew text as it was then used in the synagogue. The second column was a transliteration of the first, so that those who did not know Hebrew would at least know how it was pronounced. The other columns were occupied by various Greek translations: the Septuagint (LXX) and the translations of Aquila, Symmachus, and Theodotion. On the text of the LXX, Origen added symbols throughout to indicate different sorts of variants—additions, omissions, and so on. The work was so voluminous that no copies existed, and the text itself, preserved in Caesarea for centuries, disappeared in the seventh century, or perhaps earlier.

Later, particularly beginning in the sixteenth century, many "critical editions" of the Bible appeared. Again, this does not mean that the Bible is criticized, but rather that these are editions that, employing critical judgment, seek to determine the original text and that include notes alerting the reader to the main variants existing among ancient manuscripts and translations.

CHAPTER 6

From Manuscripts to Printed Bibles

Very little is known about the process whereby the most ancient Christian books were at first copied and circulated. One may well imagine that when Paul told the Colossians to share his epistle with the church in Laodicea, the church in Colossae, rather than sending on to Laodicea the letter they had received, would make a copy and keep the original. Likewise, when John's messenger who carried the book of Revelation to the seven churches of Asia Minor left Ephesus to continue his journey to Smyrna, believers in Ephesus would have made sure they kept a copy of the whole book. And the church in Smyrna as well as those in other cities would do the same. The wide circulation that the epistles of Paul soon achieved, as well as that of the Gospels, and then of other Christian literature, is proof that there was much activity in copying and circulating documents considered valuable. But even so, little is known about the details of this process.

When one examines the extant fragments of biblical books dating from the second century, it is clear that some of the early Christian manuscripts were written by professional or at least well-trained scribes, while others were the work of less capable copyists. However, when we come to the fourth century, there is no doubt that Christian manuscripts are the work of very able scribes. This is true of all the extensive manuscripts of that time.

From an early date there was also an interest in producing and distributing as many copies as possible of Scripture and of other Christian writings. The great polemics that took place during the second century regarding the very essence of Christian faith required the production of sufficient copies of any polemical writing to make an impact on the debate. Furthermore, since all copies were manuscripts, some people sought to bolster their views by circulating altered copies of authoritative texts. The only way to respond to such threats was to produce and distribute a greater number of copies of the original text. However, what is known today about how those copies were produced and distributed is very little. Historian Eusebius of Caesarea records an interesting fact when he says that a well-to-do Christian by the name of Ambrose, enthused by what he saw of the works of Origen, made provision so that Origen himself would have greater ease in writing, and also so that his works would be more widely distributed. Eusebius says:

> At that time Origen began his commentaries on the Divine Scriptures, being urged thereto by Ambrose, who employed innumerable incentives, not only exhorting him by word, but also furnishing abundant means. For he dictated to more than seven amanuenses, who relieved each other at appointed times. And he employed no fewer copyists, besides girls who were skilled in elegant writing. For all these Ambrose furnished the necessary expense in abundance, manifesting himself an inexpressible earnestness in diligence and zeal for the divine oracles. (*Church History* 6.23.1–2; *NPNF*[2] 1:271)

One may well imagine that, just as early in the third century Ambrose sought the distribution of Origen's writings, there must have been many others who made similar efforts in the propagation of the text of Scriptures. For this reason, as well as others, scholars have concluded that, at least in the main cities, there must have been organized means to copy and distribute the text of the Bible.

It is in the fourth century that this entire system for reproducing texts begins to appear in Christian documents. Most likely, that system was already in existence before the time of Constantine, although on a smaller scale. Eusebius of Caesarea quotes a letter he received from Constantine that attests to the enormous capacity of the centers devoted to copying manuscripts. Constantine wrote to Eusebius:

> It happens, through the favoring providence of God our Saviour, that great numbers have united themselves to the most holy church in the city which is called by my name. It seems, therefore, highly requisite, since that city is rapidly advancing in prosperity in all other respects, that the number of churches should also be increased. Do you, therefore, receive with all readiness my determination on this behalf. I have thought it expedient to instruct your Prudence to order fifty copies of the sacred Scriptures, the provision and use of which you know to be most needful for the instruction of the Church, to be written on prepared parchment in a legible manner, and in a convenient, portable form, by professional transcribers thoroughly practiced in their art. (*Life of Constantine* 4.36; *NPNF*[2] 1:549)

According to Eusebius's report, the imperial order was promptly filled—although he does not tell us by what means.

In the next century, ominous events took place that could easily have stopped the production and distribution of manuscripts of the Bible as well as of other ancient documents. Wave after wave of what to Greeks and Romans were "barbarian" peoples—most of them Germanic, but also others, notably the Huns—invaded the western areas of the Roman Empire. Cities were sacked, public order collapsed, and much of the knowledge of antiquity was set aside.

It was then that monasteries and convents, whose numbers were beginning to multiply in western Europe, came to play an important role in the history of the transmission of the sacred texts. In the year 531, Cassiodorus—whose full name was Magnus Aurelius Cassiodorus Senator—founded in Vivarium, in southern Italy, a monastery that differed from most earlier ones. He was a man of letters and a high official in the service of Ostrogoth kings. He bemoaned the loss of ancient knowledge and was convinced of the absolute importance of reading and studying Scripture. Writing about the work of one of his monks, he said, "Copying the words of the Lord will fill him with Scripture. While with his fingers he provides life for others, he also arms himself against the wiles of the devil. What he now . . . copies in his cell will be widely scattered into distant areas. He multiplies the heavenly words, and I daresay that the three fingers of his right hand repeat the very words of the most holy Trinity" (*Institutes of Divine Letters* 30). In other words, copying manuscripts, particularly those of Scripture, came to be an important part both of the devotional life of those monastics and of their mission to the rest of the world.

However, what Cassiodorus proposed would have been of much lesser impact had it not been that a few years earlier, Benedict of Nursia had founded in Monte Cassino (also in Italy) a monastery to which he gave a Rule, or constitution, that would soon be followed by the vast majority of western European monasteries. In that Rule, Benedict set the task of reading as part of monastic life, and he ordered particularly that during Lent monks be given ample time to read aloud. Although Benedict himself does not seem to have had this in mind, soon this instruction turned the monks of Monte Cassino to the task that Cassiodorus had proposed. Benedictine monasteries throughout western Europe became centers for the production of numerous copies of various texts, most of them Scripture. This was true not only of male Benedictines but also of Benedictine nuns, to the point that some of their convents became famous for the quality and beauty of their manuscripts.

The area within the monastic house where these books were produced was called the "scriptorium." There has been much discussion about exactly what these were. The most common view is that there were large rooms where monks would gather to produce their manuscripts. But apparently some scriptoria were simply small individual cells with a window to let light in, and others seem to have been set in corridors or other similar spaces within the monastery. There has also been some discussion as to whether it was common for a monk to read the manuscript aloud and have others write what he said. In most cases each copyist would work alone on a particular text. When it was necessary to produce a text in greater haste, scribes would dole out among themselves the pages to be copied. This is the main reason why there are manuscripts that have obviously been written by several different hands.

There were more tasks involved in the production of manuscripts than simply copying texts. At least until the eleventh century, papyrus continued being the material of choice for many documents. However, since papyrus itself was not very durable, monks and nuns copying manuscripts of Scripture preferred to use parchment. This was usually produced in the monastery or convent, sometimes by the copyists themselves and sometimes by others with lesser writing skills.

Also, since the copying of these texts was an act of devotion, it soon became common to adorn the manuscripts in such a way as to make them seem more worthy of their contents. One of the early means of doing this was through the application of gold, and sometimes silver. This made it appear as if the manuscripts irradiated light, and therefore this task of adorning manuscripts came to be known as "illumination," even when other colors were added. In some cases such illumination was limited to the edges of a page and consisted of vines, flowers, and the like. Quite often the illumination included the capital letter at the beginning of each section of a document, which was then decorated in many colors and usually with a painting that alluded to the text itself. The task of manuscript illumination became a specialty of some particularly gifted monastics, who would often consult with the copyists about the content of the text and how best to illustrate it.

Beginning in the twelfth century, particularly in the thirteenth, there was an explosion in studies that led to, among several other things, the founding of the oldest European universities. This increased the need for more and more affordable manuscripts, thus making ancient texts more accessible to students as well as to professors and to the wider reading public. It was apparently in connection with the universities of Paris and Bologna that the first businesses appeared that were devoted to producing manuscripts for this new market. The process was slow but inevitable. At first the most common practice was to not produce a manuscript until it was ordered by a prospective buyer. But soon the high demand for certain books led to the practice of producing manuscripts that would be ready for sale whenever someone wished to buy them. The need to produce more copies of the same books at a faster pace led to the practice of one person reading the text aloud while several others copied it.

These manuscripts produced for the new market were of lesser quality than those the monasteries and convents still produced. The latter still had beautiful illumination, and they were written on parchment. Now, just as the demand for books was increasing, a new product appeared on the scene that would greatly decrease the cost of books: paper.

Although the word "paper" derives from "papyrus," true paper, which made its way into western Europe at this time, was made not of papyrus but of fibers that made it much longer lasting and easier to produce than papyrus itself. The process of paper making was invented in China, apparently in the first century CE. For a long time, the Chinese kept the process a closely guarded secret. Then, in the eighth century, the Ottoman Turks took captive a number of Chinese who were experts in the production of paper. From then on, paper became increasingly common in the Muslim world. In the twelfth century—precisely at the beginning of the great intellectual renaissance in western Europe that led to the founding of universities—Muslim Spain began producing paper. From there the production of paper made its way into the rest of Europe, and at a rapidly increasing rate, commercially produced manuscripts began using paper, while the monastic houses still produced beautiful illuminated manuscripts written, as before, on parchment.

All of this would change drastically due in part to the great upheavals brought about by the bubonic plague in the fourteenth century, and in part to the invention of the movable-type printing press in the fifteenth. Death rates during the plague were enormously high, particularly in cities and other areas where people lived close to one another, such as convents and monasteries. Studies suggest that the plague resulted in the death of almost half of all monks and nuns, and that after it passed and the population began growing again, there were so many other needs and possibilities of occupation that the number of people in monastic life never recovered. Since it was precisely these monastics who produced most of the manuscripts of high quality, these rapidly became scarce.

A century later, in 1454 or 1455, Gutenberg's Bible was published. This was one of the first books printed using the movable-type printing press, which Gutenberg had recently invented. This invention had an enormous impact, as it opened the way for a veritable flood of written materials, and in consequence also led to a rapid increase in literacy.

Although we now see the invention of the printing press as a great step forward, at that time not all agreed. For centuries monks and nuns had considered the production of manuscripts—particularly manuscripts of Scripture, but also of the writings of ancient Christians—to be a form of devotion, as we already saw in the words of Cassiodorus. Now some people devoted to monasticism saw in the invention of the printing press the loss of an important element of their spiritual lives. In 1492, almost half a century after the invention of the press, the abbot of a monastery in Germany wrote to a colleague affirming that the task of copying manuscripts was an essential aspect of monastic life, for it helped a monk understand and live the text more fully. According to that abbot, "books written on paper are paper, and as such they will soon disappear. A scribe working on parchment can be certain that his work and its text will be long-lasting" (Johannes Trithemius, *De laude scriptorium* 25).

As to the Bible itself, the impact of the printing press was twofold. On the one hand, the press now made it possible to produce Bibles or portions of it at a relatively low cost. As Gutenberg's invention was perfected, it made the sacred texts more easily accessible to the public. This was happening precisely at the time when the Protestant Reformation was advancing, with its emphasis on the authority of Scripture. The result was an ever wider distribution of the Bible that still continues to this day. This was joined with an emphasis on the reading of Scripture both in private and as families, which for most people had not been possible earlier, when manuscripts were scarce and expensive. This accessibility led to the positive result of a greater knowledge of Scripture among Christians in general. But, on the negative side, it also led to the loss of the ancient custom of reading and studying the Bible primarily in community.

The printing press had another consequence that was less noticeable but equally important. Throughout antiquity and the Middle Ages, although scholars realized there were differences among biblical and other manuscripts of ancient writings, there was not much that could be done to settle those differences. Take, for example, Origen's *Hexapla*, discussed in chapter 5. This was a monumental piece of work that took several years. And yet most of it was lost, for all that could be done with that great work was to copy it by hand, thus making way for the introduction of new errors. For this reason, ancient and medieval scholars, while aware of the variants among manuscripts, saw no reason to devote long years to producing critical editions. But now, thanks to the printing press, the careful work of a biblical scholar in seeking to restore the original text could result in a vast number of identical copies. Given these new circumstances, during the sixteenth century there were many scholars who worked on critical editions not only of Scripture but also of other documents from antiquity.

Among the many contributions of these scholars, the best known is the critical edition of the New Testament that Erasmus published in 1516. Two years earlier, under the leadership of Cardinal Francisco Jiménez de Cisneros, the Complutensian Polyglot Bible had been completed—although it was not published until 1522. Making use of these new critical editions and of the availability of the printing press, and inspired by the Protestant Reformation, the sixteenth century was notable in the production of a vast number of biblical translations into modern languages. Some of these translations were important not only for religious reasons but also because they helped shape the emerging modern languages—as was the case with Luther's translation into German and with the King James English version.

The late twentieth and early twenty-first centuries experienced a revolution parallel to the invention of the printing press, and perhaps even greater: the development of cybernetic communication and electronic books. The Bible that in times past took years to copy by hand, then weeks to print, now takes seconds to download. People can carry the Bible on their phones. They can find particular passages with a touch of the thumb. Just as the printing press, while increasing the circulation of Scripture, also brought about an increase in other reading materials that competed with it for the attention of readers, today the electronic Bible has to compete with an almost incredible variety of other materials. Thus, the church today is faced with opportunities and challenges similar to those resulting from the invention of the printing press.

2

THE USE OF THE BIBLE

CHAPTER 7

The Reading and Use of
the Bible in Worship

A t first, all Christians were Jews, and therefore Jewish worship was the cradle within which Christian worship was shaped. In the time of Jesus, the temple was the center of Jewish religion, at least in theory. It was only there that ritual sacrifices could be made to the God of Israel. Furthermore, when praying, no matter where they were, Jews had a tradition of doing so facing the temple. The temple was particularly important for the Sadducees, who were closely linked with the aristocracy as well as with the priesthood and its leaders. The other key place of Jewish religious life was the local synagogue, which was particularly important for Pharisees. Unlike the temple, the synagogue was a place not of sacrifice but of study, prayer, and praise. Because there were many throughout the region, synagogues could be attended repeatedly and easily, whereas regular temple worship was available only to those who lived in Jerusalem or nearby and could therefore attend with relative ease. Thus, in practical terms, among Jews in the Dispersion—as well as among those who lived in the Holy Land but not near Jerusalem—the synagogue was the real center of their faith.

These conditions, which were already in existence in the times of Jesus and Paul, became inevitable after the destruction of the temple in 70 CE. After that time, synagogues were the only places where Jews would gather regularly for worship, other than in family units for prayer and religious celebrations. As a result, it was mostly the tradition of the Pharisees that shaped Judaism from that time on. Synagogue worship was centered on the study of Scripture and frequently referred to the biblical narrative—especially to the liberation from Egypt and the years in the desert. Communal prayer also took place in the synagogue but more primarily in the home, particularly in the rites accompanying the Sabbath and leading to the Sabbath meal. Such family prayers and acts of remembrance had an important place in Jewish worship and identity. After the temple was destroyed by the Romans, and when in the second century another failed rebellion led to a greater dispersion of the people of Israel, it was the synagogues and the readings and rites that took place within families that supported the identity of a people who no longer had a land base.

Things were different with Christians. During their first few generations, most frequently a conversion of a Jew to Christianity did not lead to greater family unity, but rather to anger, fear, and conflict. Christianity was seen as a fanatical sect. If a member of the family became a Christian, the family would frequently disown them. As a result, early Christians did not develop family worship as a tradition akin to that which was so important among the people of Israel.

Since it was in the synagogue that early Christian missionaries such as Paul preached the gospel of Jesus, it was synagogue worship that left its deepest mark on Christian worship. At this point it is necessary to acknowledge that little is known about the details of synagogue worship in the first century. The most ancient documents detailing such worship date from the ninth century CE, and therefore it is impossible to determine which parallelisms between worship in the synagogue and worship in the church are a result of Christians carrying over what they had done in the synagogue, and which—if any—are practices that the synagogue adopted from the church. However, there is no doubt that the focal point of synagogue worship was always the reading of Scripture, followed by an interpretation of or preaching on the sacred texts—a pattern that the ancient church continued.

This may be seen in various passages of the New Testament. One such case is Luke 4:16-21. There, we are told that Jesus read a passage in Isaiah and then "rolled up the scroll, gave it back to the attendant, and sat down. The eyes of all in the synagogue were fixed on him." The act of sitting does not necessarily mean that he returned to his place, as we might imagine today, but probably that he sat at the place from which the meaning of the passage was expounded. In Acts we have similar cases. The clearest of these appears in Acts 13:13-41, where "after the reading of the law and the prophets" Paul—in this case standing rather than sitting—interprets the Scripture readings in the light of his message regarding the Christ. This practice continued among Christians even after they were expelled from the synagogue. In 1 Timothy 4:13, there is an expectation that the churches "give attention to the public reading of scripture, to exhorting, to teaching." Although the Greek text actually says only "the reading," the NRSV is right in translating this as "the public reading." It should also be noted that in the passage itself, this reading leads to exhortation and teaching.

Formed as they were within the synagogue tradition, early Christians continued devoting time in their own worship to the reading and exposition of Scripture. At first readings were taken from what today we call the Old Testament—that is, the Hebrew Scriptures. But Christian materials were also read. When a church received a document such as a letter from Paul, it was read aloud before the congregation. The book of Revelation refers directly to the person who was to conduct this public reading (Rev. 1:3). Once they were read, some of these documents or messages would be sent to other churches, who would also read them in their own worship, as Paul himself suggests in Colossians 4:16. Also, at least by the second century, there were readings of what Justin calls the "memoirs of the apostles"—that is, the Gospels.

Just as in their physical aspect the Bibles we have today are quite different from those of early Christians, there was also a different understanding of what was meant by "reading Scripture." When today we are told we should read the Bible, what we normally understand is that we should set aside some time to read Scripture in private, possibly as part of our daily devotions. In antiquity, and even throughout the Middle Ages, very few people could read the Bible privately, for several reasons. The first such reason was the high index of illiteracy. It is impossible to know exactly what proportion of the total population of the Roman Empire was illiterate, but the most optimistic calculations suggest that less than a fifth of the population, and most likely less than a tenth, was able to read. Among this technically literate population, many could read only as much as was necessary for their own occupations or businesses. Therefore, although such people were able to read short notices having to do with their affairs, trade, etcetera, it would be difficult for them to read extensive documents such as are found in the Bible. It is possible that the index of literacy was higher among Jews than among the rest of the population. This would have to do with the importance of reading and studying the sacred texts. Since very rapidly the church was no longer composed mostly of people of Jewish origin, but rather of gentiles converted to Christianity, any advantage early Christians may have had regarding literacy would have been lost in later generations. What did remain was the Hebrew tradition regarding the central place of the written text in worship.

Another reason why people were not likely to read alone at home had to do with the manner in which manuscripts were written. The most ancient manuscripts we have of the New Testament are all written in capital letters with no separation between words and without the aid of the punctuation signs we have today. It was much later, in the ninth and tenth centuries, and originally within the Byzantine Empire, that the use of lowercase letters became common, thus facilitating reading. As for punctuation signs, apparently the first person to suggest their use was Aristophanes in the third century before Christ. But few accepted his suggestion. Much later, in the seventh century CE, Isidore of Seville made a similar attempt, but again with scant results. It was only after printed books became more common, beginning in the fifteenth century, that punctuation signs similar to what we have today were commonly used. Therefore, in antiquity, reading a text implied determining where one word ended and another began, as well as where a sentence ended. There were also no question marks or other similar punctuation indicating the inflection of a particular phrase or sentence. To make things more difficult, Hebrew manuscripts had no vowels, for the markings that represent them today in Hebrew Bibles were only introduced during the Middle Ages. Therefore, in order to read a Hebrew text, it was necessary to have some idea of what it was saying. One had to read it ahead of time and carefully to determine its meaning. For Jewish readers, whose text included no vowels, the task would be something similar as for us to read the following in English:

NTHBGNNGGDMDHVNNDRTH

Greek did include vowels, but again without punctuation or separation between one word and the next. Therefore, although Greek was easier to read, it still required a careful study of a text before reading it in public. It would be like reading:

INTHEBEGINNINGGODMADEHEAVENANDEARTH

Obviously, it would be much easier to read this line if the words were separated. If it were a longer passage, punctuation would also be helpful. The result was that most readers, no matter how skilled, had to look at a text more than once to decide on its meaning and the inflection appropriate to each phrase. This meant that, even in private, reading was usually aloud, for it was upon hearing the sound of a writing that its meaning could be understood. In the fourth century, Augustine marveled that Ambrose was able to read in silence, without pronouncing what he read—"by looking at the pages, usually understanding the meaning without saying a word nor even moving his tongue. Sometimes I was there . . . I always saw him read quietly, and never in another way" (*Confessions* 6.3.3). This implies that even Augustine, who was already a professor of rhetoric when he met Ambrose, was not able to read without pronouncing the words of the text.

A third difficulty was the scarcity of books themselves. Everything had to be copied by hand. Among the limited number of people who were able to read, very few had the dexterity necessary to write. Even so, copying a book was a long process. Therefore, books did not abound. It is quite likely that in ancient times some synagogues did not even have an entire copy of the Hebrew Scriptures. The same seems to have been true of Christian churches, at least for some time.

A final factor to be added is the growing number of "barbarians"—that is, people who were not at home in Greco-Roman culture—who would join the church. When Christianity was beginning to spread, most of these people lived beyond the borders of the Roman Empire, even though some had crossed those borders and settled in Roman territory. But among those classified as "barbarians," many others were simply descendants of the ancient inhabitants of the lands conquered by the Macedonians and the Romans who never learned the languages of their Greek or Latin conquerors. In Acts 14:8-18 we find an episode in the city of Lystra, where apparently most of the population did not understand the Greek that Paul and Barnabas spoke, for they still kept their ancient Lycaonian language. After the miraculous healing of a man who had been unable to walk since birth, "when the crowds saw what Paul had done, they shouted in the Lycaonian language, 'The gods have come down to us in human form!'" The difficulty in communicating with the inhabitants of the area was such that Paul and Barnabas were hardly able to keep people there from offering them sacrifices. Somewhat later, near the end of the second century, Irenaeus tells of a similar experience, for although he lived in what today is southern France—an area that had long been part of the Roman Empire—many of the people there were of Celtic origin and still spoke their ancient language. He says:

> To which course [the teaching of the church] many nations of those barbarians who believe in Christ do assent, having salvation written in their hearts by the Spirit, without paper or ink, and, carefully preserving the ancient tradition, believing in one God, the Creator of heaven and earth, and all things therein, by means of Christ Jesus, the Son of God; who, because of His surpassing love towards His creation, condescended to be born of the virgin, He Himself uniting man through Himself to God, and having suffered under Pontius Pilate, and rising again, and having been received up in splendour, shall come in glory, the Saviour of those who are saved, and the Judge of those who are judged, and sending into eternal fire those who transform the truth, and despise His Father and His advent. Those who, in the absence of written documents, have believed this faith, are barbar-

ians, so far as regards our language; but as regards doctrine, manner, and tenor of life, they are, because of faith, very wise indeed; and they do please God, ordering their conversation in all righteousness, chastity, and wisdom. (*Against Heresies* 3.4.2; *ANF* 1:417)

Still later, vast numbers of "barbarians" from beyond the borders of the empire would invade it and establish several semi-independent kingdoms. These invasions would not become overwhelming until the end of the fourth century and the beginning of the fifth. Such circumstances would make the reading and interpretation of Scripture much more difficult than it had been earlier. It would eventually lead to less public reading and interpretation of Scripture.

However, both before and after those invasions, when Christians spoke of "reading" the Bible, they normally meant reading it aloud within the context of worship. There are several references to this in the biblical text itself. Revelation 1:3 says, "Blessed is the one who reads aloud the words of this prophecy, and blessed are those who hear." Although the Greek says only "reads," given the context, the NRSV correctly translates it as "reads aloud." In Colossians 4:16 there are similarly clear instructions regarding this public reading: "when this letter has been read among you, have it read also in the church of the Laodiceans; and see that you read also the letter from Laodicea." And in 1 Thessalonians 5:27 Paul says, "I solemnly command you by the Lord that this letter be read to all of them [the brothers and sisters]."

In summary, most believers knew the Bible not because they had read it themselves—which most could not do—but because they had heard it read to the congregation of the faithful. Although this may surprise us today, it actually reflects the original use for which most biblical books were intended, for they were written in order to be read aloud to the people—be it the people of Israel, as in the Old Testament, or the church, as in the New.

This means the "readers" had an important role within the life of the church. One could not simply ask someone to read the Bible without previous preparation, as some do today. That task had to be assigned beforehand to people who were experienced readers, who would then take the necessary time to study the passage and eventually read it before the congregation. Thus, from the very beginning Christian worship paid particular attention both to the reading of the Bible and to those who were to read it. This followed a practice of long standing in the synagogue. As more and more gentiles joined the church, bringing with them their total ignorance of the Judeo-Christian tradition, increasing time had to be devoted to the reading and exposition of Scripture so that these former pagans could learn about creation, about the mighty works of the God of Israel, about captivity in Egypt and liberation from it, the commandments of God, the teachings of the prophets, and so forth. This is the background of the "service of the Word" to which I will refer in more detail further on. The church gave increasing prestige to those who read the Bible in worship. By the third century we begin to find Christian epitaphs declaring that the deceased—apparently all males—had been a "reader," and using that word as an honorific title.

Even before that time, there is a passage in which Tertullian, late in the second century or early in the third, speaks of "reader" as a title parallel to those of "presbyter" and "deacon." Trying to show the disorder reigning among those whom he considers heretics, Tertullian says they constantly change their bishops, and that "today one man is bishop, tomorrow another; today he is a deacon, tomorrow a reader; today he is a presbyter, tomorrow he is a layman" (*Prescription against Heretics* 41; *ANF* 3:263). Somewhat later Hippolytus, while recognizing the title of "reader," says presbyters and deacons are to be ordained with the imposition of hands, while "widows," "virgins," and "readers" are not. According to him, "a reader is named when the bishop gives him the book; but he is not ordained" (*Apostolic Tradition* 1.12).

In the year 250, Cyprian, at the time bishop of Carthage, issued the following notification:

> Know, then, that I have made Saturus a reader, and Optatus, the confessor, a sub-deacon; whom already, by the general advice, we had made next to the clergy, in having entrusted to Saturus on Easter-day, once and again, the reading; and when with the teacher-presbyters we were carefully trying readers—in appointing Optatus from among the readers to be a teacher of the hearers; examining, first of all, whether all things were found fitting in them, which ought to be found in such as were in preparation for the clerical office. (Epistle 23 [39 in Oxford edition]; *ANF* 5:301)

On the matter of readers, this passage is interesting for several reasons. Not only does it say that readers are now ordained, but it also seems to give them other functions, particularly having to do with the instruction of those preparing for baptism—the catechumens. Apparently, there were some presbyters devoted to such instruction, but readers also took part in it. One may well suppose that, since they had to work with the sacred text not only at the time of worship, when everyone heard them, but also beforehand, carefully studying the passages they were to read, readers became known as having a particular knowledge of Scripture and therefore as people to be trusted with the instruction of catechumens.

A vast number of ancient witnesses leads to the conclusion that generally Christian worship had two parts, which were eventually given the names "the service of the Word" and "the service of the Table." The former could well last several hours, during which, besides prayer and praise to God, most of the time was devoted to the reading, explanation, and application of vast passages of Scripture. The latter was the service of Communion. In general, the former followed the pattern of the synagogue, although it was much more extensive than synagogue worship because now it was necessary to educate a gentile congregation who had come to the gospel with little knowledge of Hebrew tradition or its doctrinal and moral principles. It was mostly in this part of the service that the Bible played a central role. In the second part of worship, the service of the Table, only baptized Christians could be present, for the others would have been dismissed at the end of the service of the Word. Although in this latter part of worship there were again many biblical references, the central activity was not Bible study, but rather the sharing of the Lord's Supper. (Some scholars suggest that, just as the service of the Word reflected worship practices of the synagogue, the service of the Table reflected Jewish temple worship. As a sign of this they cite the use of the word "sacrifice" in referring to the elements that believers brought to the Supper. This word appears as early as the Didache, a Christian document that may well date from the late first century. In it we find the claim that Communion is the sacrifice that the prophets announced would take place everywhere and at all times—that is, no longer just in the temple, but throughout the world [14.3].)

Some ancient texts lead us to believe that these two services, or acts of worship, were celebrated consecutively, in a single meeting. In the aforementioned passage from Justin about readings from the "memoirs of the apostles" and the prophets, Justin goes on to say that once this is done, the one presiding speaks (preaches or explains Scripture), and this is followed by Communion. But in the letter that Governor Pliny the Younger wrote to Emperor Trajan around the year 112 (and therefore some forty years before Justin), Pliny says that Christians gathered first in order to sing antiphonally to Christ as to God and to commit themselves to good behavior, and that they would then disband in order to gather again later for a shared meal. It would thus appear that practices varied according to local circumstances, and that it was later that the practice would become universal of having a single meeting that included first the service of the Word, and then—after the dismissal of those who were not ready to partake in Communion—the service of the Table.

It is the first of these two that interests us at this point, for this was the main opportunity for church members as well as candidates for baptism and others to listen to the reading of Scripture. Normally this service would include prayers as well as singing, but at its core were extensive readings of Scripture followed by a homily or an explanation of what had been read and of its importance for Christian life. Since people did not have watches, it was difficult to determine the exact time when this service would begin. Apparently, believers would dribble in as the time for the service approached. At least in some places, during this period of waiting for the rest of the congregation to arrive, someone would be reading the Bible—normally the Hebrew Bible—for those who were already there.

When speaking about the Hebrew Bible, it is important to remember that when Christianity appeared on the scene, the Old Testament canon had not been fully determined. Certainly, the five books of the Law and the books of the Prophets were considered sacred Scripture. But as to the third category, the "Writings," there were still differences of opinion among Jews. It was precisely during the first decades of Christian preaching that Judaism, after a long process, arrived at the biblical canon that is now known as the Hebrew Bible. Since most Christians did not use or read the Bible in Hebrew, but rather in the Greek translation known as the Septuagint (LXX), and this included books that did not make it into the Hebrew canon, there were books of Jewish origin that were read in church but that were not part of the Hebrew canon; these are the books that today are called "deuterocanonical," as explained in chapter 1.

We also know the service could include the reading of letters from other churches, as well as from absent leaders. We have abundant examples in the case of Paul and his epistles, as well as in the Revelation of John. But there are also other letters that were written to be read to church congregations. Late in the first century—at approximately the same time John was writing the book of Revelation—the church of Rome, under the leadership of its bishop, Clement, wrote to the Corinthians a letter calling them to unity; and it was clearly expected that this letter would be read to the entire congregation. Somewhat later Ignatius of Antioch, on his way to martyrdom in Rome, wrote seven letters—one addressed to the Christian community in Rome, another to Polycarp of Smyrna, and five to various churches (see chapter 2).

Just as the list of books in the Hebrew Bible was still in process, so the canon of the New Testament was also being shaped. From an early date the service of the Word included reading the Gospels as well as the letters of Paul and other writings, as we have already seen. At first there was no attempt to make a list of Christian books that should be read in church as part of the service. But, particularly since there were a number of books circulating whose doctrines differed from those of most Christians, a process began whereby it was eventually determined which of the most ancient Christian books should be read in church as Scripture, and which not. In the process, the two main criteria for rejecting a book were its heterodox doctrine and its late date. Since these two criteria usually coincided, it was fairly easy for most Christians to reject certain books.

Readings during the service of the Word would take several hours. Usually, a book was read in order, from one end to the other. If this could not be done in a single day, it was done in a succession of meetings. This practice of seriatim reading stood for quite some time. This is why today we have several ancient biblical commentaries that are in truth series of homilies preached on successive occasions. Someone—sometimes the preacher himself, and sometimes a hearer taking notes—collected them and turned the series of homilies and explanations into a biblical commentary.

As to the manner in which these texts were read, most probably it imitated the practice of the synagogues, where readings took the form of plainchant so that what was being said could be more easily heard and understood from afar. This sort of reading may be at the root of the custom, quite common beginning in the fourth century, of singing Scripture in plainchant.

In the most ancient church whose ruins have survived (the church in Dura-Europos in Syria), there was in the main meeting room a small platform from which the person reading or speaking could address the congregation. This was a common feature in ancient churches. This platform usually included a lectern where the book to be read was placed. Some ancient art depicts the reader seated while reading. This is not surprising, since, as already mentioned, the reading and exposition of Scripture could sometimes take several hours. In some ancient churches the speaker's platform was set off with a balustrade or similar structure. In Latin, a stage or platform for a speaker or an actor was called a *pulpitum*, and this is the origin of the English word "pulpit."

In addition to performing the public reading in worship, readers also had the responsibility of caring for manuscripts. We know, for instance, that when the mayor of Cirta in North Africa, following an imperial order to confiscate all Christian Scriptures, demanded that the bishop Paul surrender the sacred texts, the bishop answered, "The readers have our texts."

As Justin shows, the person interpreting what was read and applying it to the life of the congregation was not the reader but the bishop or pastor—or, in Justin's words, "the one presiding." We know of illiterate bishops who apparently listened to the reading of the text before the congregation by the assigned reader and who would then comment on it in the homily. However, despite such exceptions, since an important task for a pastor or bishop was to explain Scripture through preaching, soon the ability to read became an almost universal requirement to be ordained.

When, beginning with Constantine's reign early in the fourth century, the ranks of the church swelled, the best means church leaders had to instruct this vast population was preaching in the service of the Word. As a result, we have abundant sermons from the fourth and early fifth centuries from preachers such as Augustine, John Chrysostom, and others. These sermons were mostly expositions of Scripture, often beginning from one of the Gospels and then showing its relation to the whole of biblical history, and at other times devoting several weeks to the reading and exposition of a single book of the Bible.

Slowly, however, the study, preaching, and exposition of Scripture began losing its importance as the emphasis was placed more and more on the service of the Table. Throughout the Latin-speaking world, this decline was happening beginning at least as far back as the sixth century and, with a few exceptions, continuing until the sixteenth. This is probably due to the growing view that Communion itself was a miracle in which bread and wine literally became the body and blood of Christ—a miracle that eclipsed anything else to be found in the Bible itself. It was partly also due to the mass conversion of the population of the Roman Empire, followed by the invasions of peoples from beyond the Rhine and the Danube, many of them completely ignorant of Scripture. This led to a situation in which most pastors

were not able to read Scripture and explain it, and therefore had
to limit their liturgical activities to the ritual of Communion.
There were also serious difficulties in communication, for the
various invading peoples had brought with them their own languages, and, although the Latin that the conquered spoke slowly
made headway among many of the conquerors, it was difficult
to preach and explain Scripture in such a way that the people
could understand. As a consequence, the study and exposition
of the Bible in worship was now limited to special occasions such
as academic exercises in cathedral schools or, after their founding many centuries later, in universities. In the actual worship
of common people, preaching practically disappeared. There
were certainly notable exceptions and great preachers, such as
Bernard of Clairvaux; but most of the population had no opportunity to hear them regularly.

In such difficult circumstances, much of the population knew
and could recite by heart some biblical passages that were repeatedly used in liturgy, such as the songs of Mary and Simeon.
People also learned about biblical stories and events through re-
current celebrations such as Christmas and Holy Week, as well
as by means of the abundant art adorning churches, which each
generation would explain to the next. It has been said that medieval cathedrals, with their multitude of bas-reliefs and sculp-
tures, of mosaics on walls and floors, and with their multicol-
ored windows, were the storybooks of the unlearned. Many of
the people and events portrayed in the art of such churches were
biblical in origin, although these biblical figures and narratives
were often accompanied by legendary ones that were given an
authority similar to that of Scripture.

This does not mean nobody studied Scripture and meditated
on it. On the contrary, throughout the Middle Ages, particularly
beginning in the thirteenth century, there was a long tradition
of Bible study. Unfortunately, this was often limited mostly to

monastic and academic circles, and rarely appeared in the worship most people attended.

It was at the time of the Reformation that the reading and exposition of the Bible in preaching once again began occupying an important place in Sunday worship. Luther as well as Calvin and the other great Reformers, while affirming the importance of Communion, which if possible should take place every Sunday, insisted on the need for preaching on the sacred text. The recently invented printing press made it possible to distribute new translations of the Bible into the emergent languages of Europe among a population with a growing rate of literacy. Protestants found preaching particularly necessary because they felt the need to reeducate an entire population, teaching them a different way of understanding the gospel. In turn, some circles within Roman Catholicism began stressing preaching, being led mostly by the need to counteract Protestant preaching. However, it was not until much later, in the twentieth century, that the Second Vatican Council restored preaching as an essential part of Roman Catholic worship.

CHAPTER 8

The Use of Psalms

Of all the books of the Hebrew Bible, the book of Psalms is the one that is most often quoted in the New Testament. The very frequency of such quotations shows that this particular book played an important role in Christian devotion. In the New Testament there are direct references to the singing of psalms in Ephesians 3:19, Colossians 3:16, and 1 Corinthians 14:26. In Ephesians, believers are encouraged to join with others in the singing of "psalms, hymns, and spiritual songs." A similar list appears in Colossians: "sing psalms, hymns, and spiritual songs to God." The passage in 1 Corinthians seems to imply that some of these songs were a matter of personal inspiration: "each one has a hymn, a lesson, a revelation, a tongue, or an interpretation."

The Old Testament passage quoted in the New by the greatest number of authors, and repeatedly applied to Jesus, is Psalm 118:22: "The stone that the builders rejected has become the chief cornerstone." Jesus himself quotes it in connection with the parable of the wicked tenants (Matt. 21:42; Mark 12:9; Luke 20:17). When confronted by the Sanhedrin, Peter applies the same text to Jesus (Acts 4:11). And in 1 Peter 2:7 the passage is once again applied to

Jesus. In the book of Revelation there are long sections that allude to the Psalms, particularly the Hallel Psalms (Psalms 113-118).

It is important to note that early Christians, arguing with other Jews like themselves on the significance of Jesus, repeatedly quoted the Psalms and called David a prophet. The canon of the Hebrew Scriptures had not yet been completely determined, for, although the Torah and the Prophets were certainly sacred books, the collection known as the Writings was still unsettled. But Christians' frequent use of the Psalms, interpreting them as "prophecies of David" about Jesus, indicates that the authority of the Psalms was generally accepted.

There are also clear indications that in the earliest times, Christians praised the Lord both with the Psalms of Hebrew tradition and with other canticles of Christian origin. This should not surprise us, as one may surmise that during the times of Jesus and his first disciples, Jews were still composing hymns and psalms similar to those attributed to David. Some scholars suggest, for instance, that Psalm 2 was composed some one hundred years before Christ. Also, among the Dead Sea Scrolls there are manuscripts that include both canonical psalms and others that were apparently composed by the Essene community.

In the New Testament, besides the frequent quotations of the canonical psalms, there are also a number of Christian hymns. The most notable of these are to be found in Philippians 2:6-11, Colossians 1:15-20, and Hebrews 1:3. Also, particularly in the Gospel of Luke, there are several songs and poetic passages that soon became hymns sung by the ancient church—among them the song of Zechariah after the birth of John the Baptist (the Benedictus), Mary's song while visiting Elizabeth (the Magnificat), and Simeon's when Jesus is presented at the temple (the Nunc Dimittis).

Even so, little is known about the use of the book of Psalms in the primitive church. Psalms were certainly an important part of Jewish worship both in the temple and in the synagogue, and therefore Christians would continue using them. Clearly these were also songs that Jesus himself had sung while participating in synagogue worship, and from the cross he even quoted one of them. From then on, and through the centuries, the singing and recitation of Psalms have been part of Christian worship, and even today Christians are moved by realizing that the poems they are reading and repeating are ones that Jesus himself learned as a child and repeated throughout his life.

It is impossible to determine exactly how the Psalms were used in Christian worship during the first three centuries of the life of the church, when Christians lived under the menace of persecution. There is no doubt that the church continued employing in its worship the same psalms that were also used in the temple or the synagogue. There are references to this use of the Psalms in ancient authors such as Tertullian and Hippolytus; but even so, there is little that can be said about such usage. The difficulty of trying to determine how the Psalms were used in the very early church is due, first, to the lack of written testimony regarding the inner life and worship of the church during those times of persecution and, second, to a parallel lack of clear testimony as to the use of the Psalms in the synagogues of the first century. It is well known that before the destruction of the Second Temple, certain feast days were highlighted by the singing of particular psalms. But it is impossible to determine when and how the Psalms began to be used in the synagogues. It is equally impossible to determine to what extent the church did this in imitation of the synagogues, and to what extent that imitation ran in the opposite direction, synagogues seeking to compete with the church by following some of its practices. When finally the first documents appear that describe more clearly what took place both in the church and in the synagogue, there are remarkable similitudes. Most probably, early Christians, coming as they did from the synagogue and still, when possible, worshiping in it, brought the practice of singing these songs from the synagogue where they had learned them to the church in which they now gathered.

Both in synagogues and in churches, the Psalms were usually chanted not by a choir, as in the temple, but rather by a cantor to whom the congregation responded at various times by singing a short refrain, or antiphon. The exact date when this began is not clear. Christians did establish the custom of following a certain order in the use of the Psalms, which was the custom among Jews only on special occasions.

Although the question of the music that was employed has been thoroughly researched and debated, practically all that can be said is that there is a similitude between the manner in which the Psalms are sung in some of the older Jewish communities in the Middle East and traditional Christian Ambrosian, Gregorian, and Byzantine chant.

It is in the fourth century, after persecutions ended, that testimonies begin to abound regarding the use of the Psalms in Christian devotion and worship. Many examples could be cited, but the following words of Basil the Great should suffice:

> Among us the people go at night to the house of prayer, and, in distress, affliction, and continual tears, making confession to God, at last rise from their prayers and begin to sing psalms. And now, divided into two parts, they sing antiphonally with one another, thus at once confirming their study of the Gospels, and at the same time producing for themselves a heedful temper and a heart free from distraction. Afterwards they again commit the prelude of the strain to one, and the rest take it up; and so after passing the night in various psalmody, praying at intervals as the day begins to

dawn, all together, as with one voice and one heart, raise the psalm of confession to the Lord, each forming for himself his own expressions of penitence. (Epistle 207; *NPNF*² 8:247)

There is also a letter from Jerome to his colleague Eustochia consoling her after her mother's death. He tells her that in remembrance of her mother, "one after another they chanted the psalms, now in Greek, now in Latin, now in Syriac; and this not merely for the three days which elapsed before she was buried beneath the church and close to the cave of the Lord, but throughout the remainder of the week" (Epistle 108.30; *NPNF*² 6:211).

Long before these testimonies, songs had an important place in Christian devotion—a place they have kept throughout the centuries. Particularly beginning in the fourth century, the Psalms were important in three contexts: the worship service (and its impact on the population at large), monastic devotions, and private reading.

One may begin by looking at congregational worship itself. At least as early as the fourth century, for the singing of Psalms, the congregation would be divided into two groups that responded to one another. But as the congregations grew, a different responsorial form became dominant, in which a cantor would sing the text of the psalm and the congregation would respond at certain intervals with a brief phrase—or, in some cases, with the Gloria Patri ("Glory be to the Father, to the Son, and to the Holy Ghost . . ."). These congregational responses were called "antiphons" or, later, "graduals," from the word *gradum* (a step of a platform), since the cantor would stand on the steps of the pulpit to sing.

The musical ability of cantors and choir members, and their resulting prestige, came to be so important and cantors were so admired that in the year 595 a synod led by Gregory the Great declared:

In this holy Roman church a very reprehensible custom has developed, that those who are chosen for the ministry of singing are also given the ministry of the altar, for they are ordained as deacons without a careful examination of their lives, and then they devote themselves to singing, setting aside the office of preaching and neglecting support for the needy. Therefore, for the sake of a sweet voice, the matter of a life fitting the holy ministry is ignored. In this manner, while the people are delighted by a sweet voice, the wrath of God is provoked. For this reason, the present decree orders that in this church the ministers of the sacred altar shall not sing, except when reading the Gospel in a solemn mass. Psalms are to be sung by subdeacons or, if need be, by others in minor orders. (Mansi 10:3434)

As time went by and Communion eclipsed the service of the Word, there were fewer opportunities to read and explain the Psalms during the regular worship service. But there were many other occasions in which the population at large could join in the singing of the Psalms. Some of these were vigils held in the churches themselves, and others took place in monastic communities—often in the presence of the surrounding population. We do have much information regarding the singing of the Psalms in important festivities, thanks to the record left by Egeria, who late in the fourth century left her homeland of Galicia and went on pilgrimage to the Holy Land. Egeria wrote a diary that she addressed to her sisters in Spain, much of which we still have. In it she tells her sisters, for instance, that on Maundy Thursday large multitudes would spend the entire day and night, until Good Friday, in a series of services at whose core was the singing of the Psalms.

The result of all this psalm singing was that a knowledge of the Psalms was widespread among both clergy and laity. By repeating them constantly, people learned them by heart. This was of foremost importance for most believers, since they had no Bibles—and even if they had been able to have one, they would not know how to read it. For such people, memorizing the Psalms and other biblical passages was the only way they could know Scripture and meditate on it. Something similar happened with other biblical canticles that were frequently repeated—Zechariah's, Mary's, Simeon's, and others. The Second Council of Nicaea (year 787) decreed that in order to be consecrated a bishop, it was necessary to know the Psalms—which probably meant knowing them by heart.

But difficulties soon arose. Beginning in the fifth century, there were many areas where the Latin that had been commonly spoken began to decline because of the presence of various invading peoples. The church insisted on continuing to hold its services in Latin—partly seeking to salvage the unity of a Christendom that was deeply divided by different cultures—even though that language was disappearing. Thus, while the people still heard and even sang songs in Latin, and had a general idea of the meaning of what was being sung or recited, the Psalms themselves—as well as Scripture in general—lost significance in the devotional lives of the masses, who no longer spoke the language.

But even as the Psalms declined in importance among the masses, they became a central feature of much monastic devotion. In the fourth century, when Pachomius organized the first monasteries in Egypt, he instructed that monks should gather three times—at dusk, at night, and at dawn—and that at each time twelve psalms were to be recited. These psalms were recited antiphonally, a monk singing the psalm itself and the others responding by singing a brief phrase or antiphon. Other Egyptian monasteries followed similar practices. A similar program prevailed in Syria and Palestine, although the number of psalms to be sung at each period of prayer was somewhat greater. What eventually became common in the West, particularly through the influence of the Rule of Saint Benedict, was a program that included eight periods of prayer a day, with the singing of psalms in an order and at a rate that would mean the entire Psalter was sung each week. In those lands where Latin had been traditionally spoken, the constant repetition of the Psalms led monks to learn and keep some usage of Latin, so that for them the Psalms still retained their beauty and strength.

In addition, the private reading of Psalms continued throughout the Middle Ages among people of means and education. Some owned books of hours, so called because they followed the Benedictine order of prayers and psalms assigned to each hour. These often included lavish illuminations alluding to themes in the Psalms.

As previously discussed, the invention of the printing press and the Protestant Reformation democratized private access to the biblical text, including the Psalms. The Psalter was translated into several of the emerging languages of western Europe and distributed so widely that during the first fifty years after the invention of the printing press, more than three hundred editions were produced. Many of these were Catholic, and others Protestant. The main difference was that, while Catholic editions of the Psalms—as of the whole Bible—were translated from the Latin Vulgate, Protestant ones were based on the Hebrew text. Since the numbering of the Psalms according to the Septuagint, and therefore also according to the Vulgate, differed from the Hebrew numbering, a difference emerged between the numbering of Psalms in Catholic Bibles and their numbering in Protestant Bibles. The reason for this difference is that in the Septuagint and the Vulgate, Hebrew Psalms 9 and 10 are joined into one, as are also Psalms 114 and 115, while Psalms 116 and 147 are each divided in two. This results in all Bibles having 150 psalms, even though these are numbered differently. More recently some Catholic Bibles, translated directly from Hebrew, follow the Hebrew numbering and therefore coincide with Protestant Bibles. (One should note, however, that in joining Psalms 9 and 10, the Septuagint and the Vulgate were probably right, for these two psalms are actually a single acrostic poem.)

These numerous printed, mass-distributed translations of the Psalter resulted in a brief uptick in engagement with the Psalms, but in later generations the Psalms began again losing importance in the devotional life of believers, Catholic as well as Protestant. This was due partly to the decline of the earlier practice of reciting the Psalms on various occasions. It was also due to a different perspective regarding the psalms themselves, which now tended to be seen as witnesses or perhaps even as relics of the faith of ancient Israel. In contrast to this, throughout antiquity as well as the Middle Ages, the church had read the Psalms from a Christological perspective. In those earlier times, the Psalms were often interpreted as prophetic announcements about Jesus. If not, they were read as words reflecting the life and experience of Jesus himself, sometimes as if it were Jesus speaking through them.

This may be seen in the words of Augustine referring to the title at the beginning of Psalm 59:

> Several Psalms thus are marked on the face, but however in all the Passion of the Lord is foretold. Therefore here also let us perceive the Lord's Passion, and let there speak to us Christ, Head and Body. So always, or nearly always, let us hear the words of Christ from the Psalm, as that we look not only upon that Head, the one mediator between God and man, the Man Christ Jesus. . . . But let us think of Christ, Head and whole Body, a sort of entire Man. For to us is said, "But ye are the Body of Christ and members," by the Apostle Paul. If, therefore, he is Head, and we Body, then whole Christ is Head and Body. For sometimes you

find words which do not suit the Head, and unless you have attached them to the Body, your understanding will waver: again you find words which are proper for the Body, and Christ nevertheless is speaking. (*Commentary on Psalms* 59.1; BAC 246:499)

This sort of reading, both Christocentric and addressing the actual life of believers, was the main reason why throughout the Middle Ages the repetition of the Psalms and meditating on them had such importance. Furthermore, it was not only Augustine and his generation who read the Psalms in this manner. Eight centuries later, Thomas Aquinas held the same view. And even three more centuries after Aquinas, Martin Luther and John Calvin understood the Psalms in a similar manner. The latter said it quite clearly:

I have been accustomed to call this book [the Psalms], I think not inappropriately, "An Anatomy of all the Parts of the Soul"; for there is not an emotion of which any one can be conscious that is not here represented as in a mirror. Or rather, the Holy Spirit has here drawn to the life all the griefs, sorrows, fears, doubts, hopes, cares, perplexities, in short, all the distracting emotions with which the minds of men are wont to be agitated. The other parts of Scripture contain the commandments which God enjoined his servants to announce to us. But here the prophets themselves, seeing they are exhibited to us as speaking to God, and laying open all their inmost thoughts and affections, to call, or rather draw, each of us to the examination of himself in particulars in order that none of the many infirmities to which we are subject, and of the many vices with which we abound, may remain concealed. It is certainly a rare and singular advantage, when all lurking places are discovered, and the heart is brought into the light, purged from that most baneful infection, hypocrisy. In short, as calling upon God is one of the principal means of securing our safety, and as a better and more unerring rule for guiding us in this exercise cannot be found elsewhere than in The Psalms, it follows, that in proportion to the proficiency which a man shall have attained in understanding them, will be his knowledge of the most important part of celestial doctrine. Genuine and earnest prayer proceeds first from a sense of our need, and next, from faith in the promises of God. (*Commentary on Psalms*, preface, in *Calvin's Commentaries*, vol. 4 [Grand Rapids: Baker Book House, 1979], xxxvi–xxxvii)

Not only Luther and Calvin but also the other Reformers and their successors set great value on the Psalms. Several of them produced poetic translations of the Psalms, some of which became quite popular. The best known among them is the translation and adaptation Martin Luther wrote of Psalm 46, now known as the hymn "A Mighty Fortress Is Our God." Several other psalms are still particularly popular among present-day Christians, among them Psalm 100, but above all Psalm 23. However, in abandoning the Christocentric interpretation that Augustine proposes in the passage quoted above—which was the most common interpretation through the centuries—many believers of more recent generations hardly know other psalms, and consider many of them of little relevance for more modern conditions. Perhaps were we to recover that Christocentric reading of our ancestors in the faith, we would discover in the Psalms dimensions that we frequently miss. There are signs that this is beginning to happen.

CHAPTER 9

Private Reading

Although we have already affirmed that throughout antiquity the vast majority of Bible reading took place in public and in the context of worship, it is important to remember that there were also people who read Scripture on their own, either privately or in the company of their families. Given its context, such reading is much more difficult to study and document. It is clear that the reading and study of the Bible in private or within the context of the family was limited for three main reasons. The first was the already mentioned low level of literacy. The second was the difficulty in obtaining manuscripts, which required one first to borrow a text to be copied and then to have a good scribe to produce a new manuscript—or to be able to copy it oneself. (There are documented cases of people who were able to read with some difficulty but who could not write at all. The latter activity requires not only knowing the letters but also developing the muscular dexterity to put them down in writing.) A third reason why early Christians did not often read the Bible within family contexts was that many of them were members of a pagan family in which they had little authority—for instance, slaves of pagan masters or women subject to the will of pagan husbands or fathers. Such conditions would make the reading of the Bible within the context of the family, as we would understand it today, quite difficult.

These various factors were intertwined, each strengthening the others. If there were not enough manuscripts to read, there was no reason for learning to read. If having a manuscript could cause difficulties within the family—which at that time included all relatives subject to the paterfamilias as well as his slaves, and even freedmen, who were called "clients"—it was best not to have such a manuscript. If in a family some were Christians but the paterfamilias insisted on his paganism, those who embraced Christianity had to be careful before they attempted to read something the paterfamilias did not approve of.

Despite all this, we know of believers who would read in private at least portions of Scripture. On this matter, the most ancient witness we have appears in the *Church History* of Eusebius of Caesarea, as he refers to the writings of Melito of Sardis. Eusebius quotes from a letter of Melito to a certain Onesimus, written early in the second century:

> Melito to his brother Onesimus, greeting: Since thou hast often, in thy zeal for the word, expressed a wish to have extracts made from the Law and the Prophets concerning the Saviour, and concerning our entire faith, and hast also desired to have an accurate statement of the ancient book, as regards their number and their order, I have endeavored to perform the task, knowing thy zeal for the faith, and thy desire to gain information in regard to the word, and knowing that thou, in thy yearning after God, esteemest these things above all else, struggling to attain eternal salvation. (Quoted in Eusebius, *Church History* 4.26.13; NPNF[2] 1:206)

Melito then offers a list of books of the Old Testament that includes some deuterocanonical books, but not all. Much more interesting in this quote are the summaries or extracts to which Melito refers. Toward the end of the paragraph, after speaking of the books of the Old Testament, Melito adds, "From which also I have made the extracts, dividing them into six books" (Eusebius, *Church History*, 4.23.14; *NPNF*[2] 1:206). Unfortunately, these summaries have disappeared—as has also most of what Melito wrote.

What were these *Summaries*, and how were they to be used? Most scholars agree that the early Christians had collections of "testimonies," or passages in the Old Testament that pointed to Jesus—a theory that has found support after the discovery in the last few decades of a number of documents that seem to reinforce it (see chapter 12). The main reason for this theory is that many ancient authors make use of the same quotations from the Old Testament, and often in the same order. Could it be then that the summaries of Melito were actually a vast collection of such testimonies? Or were they rather a summary of the entire Old Testament? It is impossible to know. And—what is of most interest to us here—to what use was Onesimus expected to put them? Was he simply a layman who was interested in having at least some summaries of Scripture that he could read at home? In that case, this is the most ancient surviving reference to Christians reading the Bible at home or in private. However, it is also possible that Onesimus was the pastor or bishop of a church who, not having the entire text of the Hebrew Scriptures, was actually asking Melito to send him whatever he could by way of summaries outlining the main elements of those Scriptures. Once again, the question must remain open.

The next reference we have to the reading of Scripture in daily life is found in the writings of Clement of Alexandria, a few decades after Melito. Referring to a believer whose faith is deep—whom Clement would call a "true gnostic"—he says that "his sacrifices are prayers, and praises, and readings in the Scriptures before meals, and psalms and hymns during meals and before bed, and prayers also again during night" (*Stromata* 7.7; *ANF* 2:357). Obviously, the people whom Clement is addressing in this writing and whom he considers "true gnostics" were not typical believers. Alexandria, where Clement lived, was the second largest city in the Roman Empire. But it certainly was first in matters of studies, philosophy, and literature, in which it greatly surpassed Rome itself. Clement moved among the intellectual elite of that great city, and he believed part of his task was to prove to that elite that Christianity was the best of all philosophies. Therefore, Clement's readers would be exceptionally educated, and his suggestion that they should read Scripture before meals does not mean this was a general practice among the Christian population.

We come then to the *Apostolic Tradition* of Hippolytus, a few decades after Clement. Here, after declaring that all should make every effort to attend the instruction offered in church, Hippolytus adds, "However, on days in which there is no such teaching, let each read their Bible at home and read what is necessary for their benefit" (4.36). Like Clement's instructions to his "true gnostics," this is surprising, for it contradicts all we know about the index of literacy within the Roman Empire as well as what we know about the availability of the Bible itself for common Christians. As in the case of Clement, this discrepancy may be at least partly explained by considering the audience Hippolytus is addressing. The rest of his *Apostolic Tradition* deals mostly with the governance of the church—what is to be done with catechumens, how baptism is to be celebrated, who will be the leaders of the church, which of their various functions require the imposition of hands and which not, and so forth. It is quite likely that among an audience receiving guidance in such matters, the literacy index would be higher than among average Christians. Furthermore, Hippolytus was writing in Rome, where literacy would have been more common than in most of the rest of the empire.

At any rate, from that time on, texts referring to the private reading on the part of believers become more abundant. Some of these refer to the Bible itself, some to various books considered valuable, or to others that ought not to be read because they are heretical. In the homilies of Origen there are repeated references to the reading of Scripture, although it is not always clear whether he is speaking of private reading or of public reading in worship. Nor is it clear whether his comments regarding the need to read the Bible are addressed to believers in general, or to a small group among them—or, in some other cases, only to those who are to expound the meaning of Scripture within the context of worship.

It is mostly after Constantine and then almost all his successors declared themselves to be Christian and began supporting the church that we find a greater number of references to the private reading of Scripture, or to the lack thereof. The *Apostolic Constitutions*, a document that may be dated to around the year 380, recommends that those who are free from physical toil and have time should visit other believers or spend their free time reading the Bible, meditating on it, or learning about it. In Augustine's narrative of his own experience of conversion in the garden in Milan, he says that on the bench in that garden there was a codex of the Epistles of Paul, and that it was this that he read when he heard the famous words "Take and read." Thus, at the very heart of Augustine's experience of conversion, and therefore of his devotional life, stood the private reading of Scripture—although we should not forget that such reading was normally done aloud, and that Augustine was astonished when he saw Ambrose reading without pronouncing what he read. Likewise, Chrysostom, Jerome, and many others repeatedly call believers to read the Bible—in several cases, to read at home.

There are no signs of a significant rise in the level of literacy as a consequence of the new order that evolved when Constantine put an end to persecutions and began supporting the church. Certainly, the multiplication of churches that now appeared in smaller towns or villages would lead to a growing number of readers and clergy, and therefore one may well imagine that the very need to read Scripture in public would result in a slight rise in the literacy index. But this would not necessarily lead to an increase in the private reading of Scripture. On the other hand, there are indications that, at least among people of means, some began having portions of Scripture that they kept at home. An interesting example are some miniature codices containing part of the sacred text. It is probably these that Chrysostom refers to when he speaks of women who carry Gospels hanging from their necks. However, the importance of such codices as a sign of the private reading of Scripture must not be exaggerated, for we also know of people who carried on their bodies a portion of the sacred text not in order to read it, but rather as a talisman. Perhaps this was done in imitation of the ancient Jewish custom of placing the sacred text on their doorways and carrying it on their bodies, per the commandment of God. Such practices seem to stand behind the words of John Chrysostom, a highly educated and eloquent preacher, who claimed that the devil would not enter into a home that was kept safe by the sacred text. Many, however, found such use of the word of God reprehensible. Years before the time of Chrysostom, in 360, a synod gathered in Laodicea ordered that clergy must refrain from producing such amulets (canon 36), which indicates that such texts were being produced, if not by clergy, at least by laity.

Apparently, the private reading of Scripture became more common in the fourth and fifth centuries as people of a higher class and therefore with more education began joining the church. Still, most common believers did not have Bibles that they could read in their own homes, but rather went to church to hear the reading of Scripture. This may be seen in the comments

Chrysostom makes regarding how little Christians knew of the Bible—comments that refer not only to the lack of reading at home but also to those who do not listen to its reading in church or pay attention to its exposition and interpretation:

> For, tell me, who of you that stand here, if he were required, could repeat one Psalm, or any other portion of the divine Scriptures? There is not one.
>
> And it is not this only that is the grievous thing, but that while ye are become so backward with respect to things spiritual, yet in regard of what belongs to Satan ye are more vehement than fire. Thus should any one be minded to ask of you songs of devils and impure effeminate melodies, he will find many that know these perfectly, and repeat them with much pleasure.
>
> But what is the answer to these charges? "I am not," you will say, "one of the monks, but I have both a wife and children, and the care of a household." Why, this is what hath ruined all, your supposing that the reading of the divine Scriptures appertains to those only, when ye need it much more than they. For they that dwell in the world, and each day receive wounds, these have most need of medicines. So that it is far worse than not reading, to account the thing even "superfluous": for these are the words of diabolical invention. (*Homilies on Matthew* 2.9; *NPNF*[1] 10:13)

CHAPTER 10

The Bible and Education

W hen dealing with the relationship between the Bible and education in the early church, one must begin by noting that, with some exceptions—particularly in Alexandria—most Christians thought that classical literature, Greek as well as Latin, was at best useless, and probably even harmful. An exception was often made for the writings of the great philosophers of antiquity, particularly of Plato, whom many saw as a bridge making it possible to preach the gospel to cultured gentiles. But works such as those of Homer, Aristophanes, Virgil, and other great literary figures of antiquity reflected the mythology and beliefs of the times and the contexts in which they were written, and therefore many early Christians believed they should not be studied or taught to new generations, who might learn from them both the idolatrous beliefs of antiquity and a host of attitudes, values, and behaviors that the church considered unacceptable. Thus, those who were in charge of the instruction of younger generations were repeatedly beseeched not to employ in their teaching such pagan works, but rather the Bible and its narratives.

On the other hand, it was impossible to live in the midst of Greco-Roman culture and not appreciate its achievements. Even the most outspoken enemies of classical culture show signs of the influence of that culture on their own thought and worldview. Tertullian, famous for his claim that Athens had nothing to do with Jerusalem, and that the academy had nothing to do with the church, was in many ways a Stoic. The impact of Platonism on Christian theology is well known, not only in Alexandria, where it was most noticeable, but even on those who rejected Platonism, such as Methodius of Olympus. Roman legal concepts and Roman jurisprudence left an imprint not just on matters of social ethics, but even on some interpretations of the Trinity. Allegorical biblical interpretation was patterned after the manner in which pagans allegorized Homer and the rest of the Greco-Roman literary canon. Ambrose and Augustine imitated Cicero's style. And the scholarly studies of Scripture by people such as Origen and Jerome followed methods that had long been employed by pagans in the study of their own literature.

Official Christian disdain for pagan literature had its counterpart in the disdain of many pagans for Christianity itself. Pagans insisted that Christians had no right to use this literature dealing with the actions of gods in which they did not believe. A typical case was that of Emperor Julian—inappropriately called "the Apostate," for in truth, although he had been baptized, he never was a Christian—who in his efforts to restore the ancient tradition forbade Christians from teaching the classical writings of Greco-Roman antiquity.

The result of this ambivalence regarding the dominant culture was that, although most Christians were not learned, and many rejected classical education as an instrument of paganism, a good number of educated Christians did not hesitate to use their pagan learning in fields such as rhetoric, philosophy, philology, and hermeneutics by applying it to their biblical studies and interpretation. Indeed, examples abound, since those who worked along these lines were also the ones who wrote most of the extant texts and who were certainly the most influential figures throughout the history of Christian thought. In antiquity, one immediately thinks of Justin, Origen, Basil, Jerome, Augustine, and Chrysostom.

If one of the purposes of education is to bring learners into the fold of a culture and a social order, one must say that, at least until Christianity became the dominant religion near the end of the fourth century, when the Bible was taught this was not done in order to help people find their place in society; it was to help the student become part of a new society, of this church that saw itself as a new people of God, a new nation. It was precisely during the last decades of the fourth century and the beginnings of the fifth that the Bible became no longer a tool for creating a different people within the surrounding society, but rather a way of encouraging and leading all members of that society to accept, live, and apply the new values and the narratives of Christian identity.

This leads us to the manner in which the Bible itself was taught. Christianity inherited from Judaism a tradition of careful study of Scripture and an emphasis on the memorization of basic passages. As we have repeatedly seen in other chapters, for several reasons most believers were not able to read the Bible. Furthermore, this was mainly an oral rather than a written culture, and in such a culture people tend to learn more by hearing and repeating a text than by reading it directly.

Given such circumstances, most of the Christian population learned the content of Scripture by hearing it read in congregational meetings and then repeating or singing some crucial texts. This meant that in worship there was a tendency to make repeated use of particular passages so that the people might learn them without ever reading them. This included not only the Lord's Prayer but also songs such as may be found in the Gospel of Luke, particularly those of Zechariah, Mary, and Simeon (traditionally known by the beginning of their Latin translations: the Benedictus, the Magnificat, and the Nunc Dimittis).

Those who arrived early at the worship service were able to listen to the reading of extensive biblical passages that, at least in some churches, were read while waiting for the rest of the congregation to arrive. In the service of the Word, the Bible was first read and then explained. This was the main means by which most Christians learned about the Bible and its teachings.

When someone wished to join the church, this was communicated to the bishop or pastor so that the person's name could be included in an official list of catechumens. The catechumens would meet regularly to learn about the faith and to study the Bible, normally under the leadership of a layperson who had been considered able and appointed for this task. This process usually took two years, and sometimes three, before the person was considered ready for baptism. Baptism itself normally took place during the night between Holy Saturday and Easter Sunday. Once baptized, the neophyte continued attending the service of the Word and therefore learning more about the Bible. It is quite likely that, following the usual practice of oral cultures, and continuing what they had learned from Jewish practice, people would memorize biblical passages and then ruminate on them in their private or family devotions.

The best Christian teachers were conscious of the need to adapt teaching in such a way that it would meet the needs and circumstances of those for whom it was intended—and, when necessary, also offer a response to common objections or preconceived ideas. Thus, Gregory of Nyssa opens his *Great Catechism* affirming this pedagogical principle:

> The presiding ministers . . . have need of a system in their instructions, in order that the Church may be replenished by the accession of such as should be saved, through the teaching of the word of Faith being brought home to the hearing of unbelievers. Not that the same method of instruction will

be suitable in the case of all who approach the word. The
catechism must be adapted to the diversities of their religious
worship; with an eye, indeed, to the one aim and end of the
system, but not using the same method of preparation in
each individual case. (prologue; *NPNF²* 5:473)

Unfortunately, as far as our interests here are concerned,
Gregory's *Great Catechism* is devoted mostly to explaining and
defending orthodox doctrine in the debates of the time regarding
the doctrine of the Trinity and Christology. As a result, the *Catechetical Lectures* of Cyril of Jerusalem, delivered in or about the
year 347, are of greater interest to us. Furthermore, Gregory's
work was addressed to "those who will be presiding," and therefore it deals more with the theory of teaching, and what he says
regarding theology is much more extensive than most catechumens would be taught. In contrast, Cyril's lectures let us see the
contents of his teaching. As was customary in many churches,
in Jerusalem Cyril devoted much of the time leading to Easter
Sunday to the final preparation of the catechumens who were to
be baptized on that day. Then, as was also customary, he continued his series of lectures with another five delivered in the days
immediately following Easter Sunday. In these final lectures he
explained to the neophytes the meaning and significance of the
baptism they had received, of the Eucharist in which they now
participated, and of several of the symbolic actions connected
with these two sacraments.

Cyril was clear about the mixed motives of those who heard
him and who claimed they sought baptism because they wished
to be united to the church. In a passage that reminds us of many
of the reasons why people attend church today, Cyril says:

Possibly too thou art come on another pretext. It is possible
that a man is wishing to pay court to a woman, and came

hither on that account. The remark applies in like manner
to women also in their turn. A slave also perhaps wishes to
please his master, and a friend his friend. I accept this bait
for the hook, and welcome thee, though thou camest with
an evil purpose, yet as one to be saved by a good hope. (*Pro-
catechesis* 5; NPNF² 7:2)

Even so, Cyril repeatedly invites those who hear him to study
and meditate on what he calls "the oracles of God"—that is, Scripture. Again, this should not lead us to the conclusion that each
of these catechumens had direct access to a written Bible. The
literacy index was still low. Cyril does expect that some of his
listeners will have direct access to a Bible, but at the same time
he is quite aware that most of them will be able to learn of the
sacred text only when it is read and discussed in church, in the
service of the Word. Therefore, in the same lecture in which he
shows he is aware that those who have come to hear him and
who seek baptism are not moved only by the best and purest
motives, Cyril exhorts:

Attend closely to the catechisings, and though we should
prolong our discourse, let not thy mind be wearied out. For
thou art receiving armour against the adverse power, armour
against heresies, against Jews, and Samaritans, and Gentiles. Thou hast many enemies; take to thee many darts, for
thou hast many to hurl them at: and thou hast need to learn
how to strike down the Greek, how to contend against heretic, against Jew and Samaritan. And the armour is ready, and
most ready *the sword of the Spirit*: but thou also must stretch
forth thy right hand with good resolution, that thou mayest
war the Lord's warfare, and overcome adverse powers, and
become invincible against every heretical attempt. (*Procat-
echesis* 10; NPNF² 7:3)

A few years after Cyril's lectures, an anonymous author—or most likely several authors—wrote the *Apostolic Constitutions*. There we find a passage implying that the intended readers of these constitutions would have direct access to the written text of Scripture, and that they would be able to use it so as to be educated—educated in the profound sense of being shaped by the Bible itself. Its readers are told:

> Abstain from all the heathen books. For what hast thou to do with such foreign discourses, or laws, or false prophets, which subvert the faith of the unstable? For what defect dost thou find in the law of God, that thou shouldest have recourse to those heathenish fables? For if thou hast a mind to read history, thou hast the books of the Kings; if books of wisdom or poetry, thou hast those of the Prophets, of Job, and the Proverbs, in which thou wilt find greater depth of sagacity than in all the heathen poets and sophisters, because these are the words of the Lord, the only wise God. If thou desirest something to sing, thou hast the Psalms; if the origin of things, thou hast Genesis; if laws and statutes, thou hast the glorious law of the Lord God. Do thou therefore utterly abstain from all strange and diabolical books. (*Apostolic Constitutions* 1.2.6; *ANF* 7:393)

At approximately the same time, or perhaps a few years later, John Chrysostom wrote the treatise *On Vainglory and the Education of Children*, in which he suggests to those in charge of the development of children—parents, tutors, servants—to make use of the innate curiosity of children to teach them the Bible:

> Therefore let them not hear frivolous and old wives' tales: "This youth kissed that maiden. The king's son and the younger daughter have done this." . . . But when the boy

takes relaxation from his studies—for the soul delights in stories of old—speak to him, drawing him away from childish folly, for thou art raising a philosopher and an athlete and citizen of heaven. Speak to him and tell him this story: "Once upon a time there were two sons of one father, even two brothers." Then after a pause continue: "And they were the children of the same mother, one being the elder, the other the younger son. The elder was a tiller of the ground, the younger a shepherd. . . ."

And let the child's mother sit by while his soul is being formed by such tales, so that she too may take part. (38-39; trans. M. L. W. Laistner, in *Christianity and Pagan Culture in the Later Roman Empire* [Ithaca, NY: Cornell University Press, 1951], pp. 102-3)

Chrysostom then goes on to advise mothers to discuss these stories with the children. Thus they will awaken the interest of their children and their understanding of Scripture, to the point that someday they will tell the story themselves and try to imitate the mother who told it to them in the first place. And then, knowing that story, they are to be told how to apply it in their own lives.

Finally, among the great thinkers of antiquity who discussed how the Bible should be taught, one must mention Augustine, who wrote the treatise *On the Instruction of the Uncultured*—that is, of those who have not had much opportunity to learn. There Augustine makes it very clear that he does not agree with those who seem to believe that the best way to teach the Bible is to have people try to learn it by heart from Genesis to Revelation. With a good measure of realism, he says that time does not suffice for doing such a thing, and that in any case it is unnecessary for all to know the Bible by heart. It is best to summarize it and to order it in such a way that the most important stories and passages can be underscored. He also suggests that it is best to begin with those texts that are more pleasing and that have attracted people in times past. This is not to be done seeking to repeat what is always said about such passages, but rather to lead those who hear to examine the passages themselves and to be surprised by all they find in them. In this manner, these crucial passages will also be important to the new learners, and memory will not be confused by excessive detail.

In summary, it is clear that in the ancient church there was a profound interest in teaching the Bible, that this was done mostly in the service of the Word, that those who had access to the written text were expected to set aside time to read it and meditate on it, and that, above all, people attending worship and therefore hearing the reading and exposition of Scripture were expected to reflect on what they had heard and on how they could and should apply it in their own lives.

Another important means of teaching Scripture was art. Both in the catacombs of Rome and in the ruins of the most ancient churches, we find the remains of frescoes that portray some of the narratives and allegories of Scripture. For instance, in the baptistery in the church of Dura-Europos there is a painting of the Good Shepherd that seems to be indicating that those who enter the baptismal waters will now be part of God's fold. Under that painting there is another representing Adam and Eve. And at other places in the same room there are representations of the Samaritan woman at the well, David and Goliath, the healing of a paralytic, Peter and Jesus walking on water, and Jonah, as well as several other paintings that have been so damaged by time that it is impossible to determine their exact subject. (Many of the paintings in the Dura-Europos baptistery have something to do with water, thus alluding to the baptisms that would take place there.) Likewise, in the Roman catacombs there are sev-eral paintings whose purpose seems to be to instruct the faithful and to remind them of the biblical passages to which they refer—paintings of Jesus with the apostles, the Good Shepherd, the three young men in the fiery furnace, and many others. Such art, in churches as well as in the catacombs, was intended not only for decoration but also and above all as a way to lead Christians to picture and remember what was read in Scripture.

Although this will carry us far beyond the chronological limits set by the title of this book, a few words about later developments are in order. Late in the fourth century and particularly during the fifth, the educational system that the church had developed began to dissolve due to new circumstances. In the fourth century the church that until then had been in constant danger of persecution became the official religion of the Roman Empire. In consequence, multitudes were now requesting baptism, and there were not sufficient believers with the necessary training to teach and advise the rapidly growing number of catechumens. The result was that the catechumenate was drastically shortened, to the point that it eventually disappeared. As if this were not enough, at the same time, particularly during the fifth century, a series of invasions swept the western regions of the empire. Most of this population would eventually adopt Christianity—some were already Arian Christians, and would later be converted to the Nicene faith. But it was still mostly an illiterate population, with the added difficulty that now most of these invaders, who now ruled a series of independent or semi-independent kingdoms, did not speak Latin—which until then had been the common language for communication throughout the western areas of the empire. Given such circumstances, practically the only centers of study that still existed were monasteries, which would eventually play an important role in the renewal of learning—and concretely, as we have already seen, in the reproduction and transmission of biblical and other manuscripts.

With a mostly illiterate population speaking a variety of languages, art came to occupy an ever-growing role in the transmission of biblical knowledge to the masses. Those who could not read about the birth, crucifixion, and resurrection of Jesus could see the entire story in mosaic, stone, paint, or glass. Soon church buildings became the people's books. This process continued, so that when we come to the time of the great medieval cathedrals, we find represented there not only biblical stories but also the stories and legends of many saints and martyrs. Even though today it is difficult for us to understand what this meant for the population, such buildings were the main means by which most medieval people came to know the Bible as well as their own history as a church. The more scholarly study of the Bible that had always characterized the church even before the time of Constantine now continued mostly in monastic establishments—both men's and women's. But such studies reached only a small minority of the population.

As a response to that situation, schools arose in monastic establishments as well as in the cathedrals of large cities. Monastic schools developed mostly because some aristocratic families took their children, particularly their sons, to be educated in a monastery. Cathedral schools developed particularly after the sixth century. Both sorts of schools grew not only in size but also in number, and became one of the most useful instruments the church had in promoting not only biblical studies but all sorts of learning.

Toward the end of the eighth century and early in the ninth, under the regime of Charlemagne and some of his successors, there was a brief renaissance in the study of letters. But it was not until the twelfth century and early in the thirteenth that the great intellectual awakening took place that would lead to the formation of universities and of scholastic theology. Most universities resulted from a fusion of cathedral and monastic schools. Those who wished to study theology, after spending several years in the study of the trivium (the "three ways": grammar, logic, and rhetoric) moved on to the quadrivium (the "four ways": astronomy, arithmetic, geometry, and music) in order then to begin their theological studies. The first degree they were awarded in such studies was that of bachelor in Bible. Such bachelors would then spend several years of further study, during which they also lectured on the sacred texts. This was followed by a long curriculum that could easily take an additional decade of studies.

All of this means that it is not true, as is often said, that the Middle Ages were a time of biblical and doctrinal ignorance. It was a time in which there was a great chasm between those who studied and those who did not. Among the former, there was little interest in sharing their knowledge with the less cultured, or in relating their studies with the actual life of the church or of the population at large. Among the latter, legends, superstitions, and general ignorance were the order of the day.

The Protestant Reformation, with the aid of the printing press, greatly changed the situation. One outstanding leader in a movement for the renewal of studies was Philip Melanchthon, Luther's younger colleague at the University of Wittenberg, who took a particular interest in education. In 1524, following a program that Melanchthon had outlined, Luther wrote a *Letter to the Councilmen of All German Cities* in which he proposed that the government should take a hand in public education by establishing and supervising schools. Luther also was convinced, as few were in his time, that education should be available not only for boys but also for girls. At any rate, the condition of most schools in existence was abysmal, and therefore the Reformation was addressed at the renewal not only of the church but also of schools and of study. According to a report by Melanchthon, there were many schoolteachers who did not even know how to read and who simply taught the students to memorize the

Creed, the Decalogue, and the Lord's Prayer. Other Reformers, such as Zwingli and Calvin, shared Melanchthon's concern for education. This was the beginning of a vast movement that eventually led to the modern conviction that public education is essentially the responsibility of the state—although one must remember that at that time it was expected that the entire population would be Christian, and therefore public education, no matter whether led by the church or by the state, would have the same content.

To this one may add that the Reformation of studies also reached the university level, and that Melanchthon proposed a curriculum that was soon adopted by several German universities. He rejected the older scholastic method, insisted on the need to know the original biblical languages, and proposed that the curriculum in theology should begin with biblical studies—specifically, with the study of Romans.

This academic Reformation grew from two sources. On the one hand, humanists had been proposing such reforms for quite some time. On the other, Melanchthon and the other Reformers saw in education an act of obedience to God. In 1552 Melanchthon reminded all that "God wrote the Decalogue in stone tablets, and ordered that the books of the prophets and apostles be studied. . . . It is necessary to have those who are able to read these books and thus learn true doctrine. . . . For the interpretation of the Bible to be correct, there must be some who, knowing the languages of the apostles and prophets, as well as anything that may contribute to their task, are able to teach others" (*Order for the Schools of Mecklenburg*).

From then on, and to this day, these two motivations—the need to promote the education of the people, and the task of letting the Bible be known—have often been merged, particularly in what is called "the mission field." In Latin America, when Scottish Baptist missionary James (Diego) Thomson landed in

Buenos Aires in 1818, he brought with him a then revolutionary method of education—the Lancaster method, so named after
one of its creators. In this method, in which each student taught
others, the fundamental text was the Bible. In his work in Latin
America, Thomson was representing not only the Lancaster
method but also the British and Foreign Bible Society. Similar
connections between education and Scripture have continued
to this day, for during the twentieth and twenty-first centuries,
millions of believers have joined literacy campaigns moved at
the same time by the need to educate the people and by the conviction that they must be able to read the Bible. In thus seeing the
Bible as both a means and an end to literacy and learning—and
seeing general education as both an end and a means to promote
biblical literacy—present-day Christians remind us of a connection between the Bible and education that was already embodied
in the educational efforts of early Christianity.

CHAPTER 11

The Bible and the Social Order

The Bible refers repeatedly, and often with strong words, to the ordering of society in all its dimensions. Much of the law of Israel is directly related to the social order. There we find, among many other instructions, laws regarding the ordering of the family and the rights of the poor, widows, orphans, and foreigners (categories of people who were generally powerless), as well as how the people of God are to be ruled. The same is true of the rest of the Hebrew Scriptures, where the prophets repeatedly call for justice, proclaim the wrath of God against those who take advantage of the helpless, and announce a new day of universal flourishing that involves the setting right of human relationships and systems. All of this is frequently echoed in books such as Psalms and Proverbs.

Coming to the New Testament, one might think that such concerns would disappear, or at least be less prominent. But that is not the case. Jesus tells his disciples that they are to "strive first for the kingdom of God and his righteousness" (Matt. 6:33). This righteousness, understood in the light of the entire biblical witness, is not the mere rectitude of each believer but also a different social order that may well be called the reign of God or a new city descending from heaven. It is important to note that both the metaphor of a kingdom and that of a city refer to social orderings. Also, there are elsewhere in the New Testament words regarding social justice that are as clear and harsh as any spoken by the ancient prophets of Israel.

On the other hand, the New Testament was written in particular social circumstances, and this may be seen in what it says regarding the ordering of society. Clearly, early Christians sought to live according to a social order that was different than that of the surrounding society. In this they were inspired by the words of Jesus: "The kings of the Gentiles lord it over them; and those in authority over them are called benefactors. But not so among you; rather the greatest among you must become like the youngest, and the leader like one who serves" (Luke 22:25-26).

While seeking to create a different order within their own community, those early Christians were unable to offer laws for the entire population, as Moses and David had done. Any prophetic voice within the church would not carry within the surrounding society the same weight that the voices of ancient prophets had. When those early Christians criticized the existing order, even when their words were as harsh as those of the ancient prophets, their words would not usually be heard by the rulers—and if they were heard, they would not be heeded.

Even under such conditions, which frequently led to persecution, few early Christians thought this was an excuse to ignore the surrounding social order. On the contrary, in the writings of the first three centuries of the life of the church, we find frequent allusions to the order of society and how the church is to relate to it. On the basis of the biblical witness, those ancient Christians expressed their concerns regarding society in at least four ways.

The first was to address the authorities—in some cases the emperors themselves—requesting the end to persecution against Christians, but also calling the government itself to a greater justice. Thus, Justin Martyr dared tell Emperor Titus about the immorality that existed under his regime, and pointed out that the emperor himself profited from that immorality:

> But as for us, we have been taught that to expose newly-born children is the part of wicked men; and this we have been taught lest we should do any one an injury, and lest we should sin against God, first, because we see that almost all so exposed (not only the girls, but also the males) are brought up to prostitution. And as the ancients are said to have reared herds of oxen, or goats, or sheep, or grazing horses, so now we see you rear children only for this shameful use; and for this pollution a multitude of females and hermaphrodites, and those who commit unmentionable iniquities, are found in every nation. And you receive the hire of these, and duty and taxes from them, whom you ought to exterminate from your realm. (*First Apology* 27; *ANF* 1:172)

Also, several Christian writers from those early centuries accused the authorities of issuing and following unjust and contradictory laws against Christians. Justin himself does this almost at the very beginning of his *First Apology*:

> Do you, then, since ye are called pious and philosophers, guardians of justice and lovers of learning, give good heed, and hearken to my address; and if ye are indeed such, it will be manifested. For we have come, not to flatter you by this writing, nor please you by our address, but to beg that you pass judgment, after an accurate and searching investigation, not flattered by prejudice or by a desire of pleasing superstitious men, nor induced by irrational impulse or evil rumours which have long been prevalent, to give a decision which will prove to be against yourselves. For as for us, we

reckon that no evil can be done us, unless we be convicted as evil-doers, or be proved to be wicked men; and you, you can kill, but not hurt us. (2; *ANF* 1:163)

A second way in which Christians expressed their concern for the ordering of society was by reflecting on the place of the existing order in God's designs, even though that unjust order persecuted Christians. Thus, even while Christians were persecuted and killed by Roman authorities, some began speaking of the much-vaunted Pax Romana—the order that the Roman Empire had brought to the entire Mediterranean basin—as part of the design of God to facilitate the expansion of Christianity. In his treatise *Against Celsus*, written in the mid-third century in defense of Christianity, the famous Christian scholar Origen presents the Pax Romana as the fulfillment of what was promised in Psalm 72:7: "In his days may righteousness flourish and peace abound":

Moreover it is certain that Jesus was born in the reign of Augustus, who, so to speak, fused together into one monarchy the many populations of the earth. Now the existence of many kingdoms would have been a hindrance to the spread of the doctrine of Jesus throughout the entire world; not only for the reasons mentioned, but also on account of the necessity of men everywhere engaging in war, and fighting on behalf of their native country, which was the case before the times of Augustus, and in periods still more remote, when necessity arose, as when the Peloponnesians and Athenians warred against each other, and other nations in like manner. How, then, was it possible for the Gospel doctrine of peace, which does not permit men to take vengeance even upon enemies, to prevail throughout the world, unless at the advent of Jesus a milder spirit had been everywhere introduced into the conduct of things? (2.30; *ANF* 4:4)

Third, early Christians expressed their social concerns by seeking to create among themselves a new order of love and justice. What Paul had said, that in Christ there is no slave nor free, became a guideline for the social ordering that the church attempted to create within itself. Although frequently what the book of Acts says about having all things in common is dismissed as a very temporary practice, ancient Christian writers abundantly show that this continued being the ideal—and often the practice—of the ancient church for at least two or three centuries. This may be found in the Didache, which may well date from the last years of the first century, and late in the second century it is repeated with practically the same words in the so-called Epistle of Barnabas:

> Thou shalt communicate [share] in all things with thy neighbour; thou shalt not call things thine own; for if ye are partakers in common of things which are incorruptible, how much more [should you be] of those things which are corruptible! . . . As far as possible, thou shalt be pure in thy soul. Do not be ready to stretch forth thy hands to take, whilst thou contractest them to give. (Pseudo-Barnabas 19; ANF 1:148)

This did not mean there was no place in the church for the rich. But those who were rich understood that their possessions had been given to them for the sake of the poor. In the middle of the second century, Hermas, whose brother was the bishop of Rome, addressed the following words to the well-to-do members in that church:

> Instead of lands, therefore, buy afflicted souls, according as each one is able, and visit widows and orphans, and do not overlook them; and spend your wealth and all your preparations, which ye received from the Lord, upon such lands and

houses. For to this end did the Master make you rich, that you might perform these services unto Him; and it is much better to purchase such lands, and possessions, and houses, as you will find in your own city, when you come to reside in it. This is a noble and sacred expenditure, attended neither with sorrow nor fear, but with joy. Do not practise the expenditure of the heathen, for it is injurious to you who are the servants of God; but practise an expenditure of your own, in which ye can rejoice; and do not corrupt nor touch what is another's nor covet it, for it is an evil thing to covet the goods of other men; but work thine own work, and thou wilt be saved. (Shepherd of Hermas, Similitude 1; *ANF* 2:31–32)

Likewise, although in the social order there were still masters and slaves, in the church masters were to receive their slaves as brothers and sisters. This should be clear from a reading of Paul's Epistle to Philemon, where he tells Philemon that he is to receive his escaped slave Onesimus "no longer as a slave but more than a slave, a beloved brother" (Philem. 16). Although in a way the letter was a request or directive to Philemon, it was also a letter to the entire church in Colossae, for Paul addresses it "To Philemon our dear friend and co-worker, to Apphia our sister, to Archippus our fellow soldier, and to the church in your house" (Philem. 1–2). Therefore, the relationship between a Christian master and a Christian slave is not merely a matter between the two of them, but rather the entire church is called to be a witness of the new order that should now exist, in which the master's slave now becomes his brother. Although there were laws making it very difficult to free slaves in an official manner, Philemon—and by extension any other Christian master—was supposed to receive his slaves as brothers and sisters.

Finally—but most importantly—Christians dealt with the social order by praying for the emperor and other rulers, even when these were persecuting them. This was usually included in

the "prayer of the faithful" that took place at the beginning of the
service of the Table. This prayer was not just one more element
within the worship service but was actually an expression of
the manner in which the church understood itself. According
to the New Testament, the church is a "royal priesthood." Immediately after baptism, every neophyte was anointed as were the
kings and priests in the Old Testament. Now, by virtue of such
anointing, this person had become part of the royal priesthood
that is the church. Part of the task of this church is then to lift all
of humankind in petition before the heavenly throne. From the
point of view of believers, this was so important that an ancient
Christian writer dared say that "what the soul is in the body, that
are Christians in the world" (To Diognetus 6.1; ANF 1:27). In other
words, just as the body cannot live without a soul, it is actually
the church, this priestly people, that makes it possible for the
world to continue in existence.

All this changed radically in the fourth century, when Constantine, and almost all his successors, favored the church. In
slightly over half a century, Christianity, until then a persecuted
religion, became practically the only faith accepted within the
empire—the main exception being Judaism. During the first two
centuries of this new situation, there was a process whereby the
social order that Christians had practiced and proclaimed had to
be adjusted to the political, economic, and social realities of the
empire. In that process of adjustment there were valiant voices
that, inspired by the prophets of old, insisted on justice for the
poor and criticized such practices as slavery. Some protested
against gladiatorial fights and even died to see those fights abolished. Others stood firm and faced emperors and their represen-
tatives, condemning their cruelty. Many of these—Athanasius,
Basil the Great, Gregory Nazianzen, Ambrose, Jerome, John
Chrysostom, and many others—eventually became well-known
saints within the church; but, significantly, this aspect of their

life and work was often forgotten as the church increasingly came to accept the existing social order of the empire.

As one thinks about those times, there are two important points to underline. On the one hand, a number of laws regarding the social order were enacted that were clearly inspired by biblical principles. One of the best-known examples is the ancient Sabbath laws inspiring similar laws, now applied on Sunday, that at least provided some rest for laborers. Another example is a long series of laws against usury.

On the other hand, the radical social reordering that was originally expected of all believers now shifted to become the responsibility of monastics, both men and women, while the common believers could ignore it, or at least discount it. Monks and nuns were now really the only ones who had all things in common. Likewise, the task of praying for all humankind originally expressed in the prayer of the faithful now became a specific task of convents and monasteries, which were praying for the rest of the world while other Christians generally went about their business. In a word, monastic life became a higher echelon of discipleship, whose participants were committed to following a social order based on what were understood to be biblical principles, while other believers were at least partially excluded from such responsibilities.

Something similar was true throughout the Middle Ages. Although there were repeated clashes between civil and ecclesiastical authorities, most of these had to do with matters of jurisdiction and authority rather than of justice within the social order. As to that order, the church tended to limit its interventions to matters of sexual morality. There were also efforts to limit the damage of continuous warfare among feudal lords through the "Peace of God" and the "Armistice of God"—ecclesiastical declarations limiting the times and places in which war was allowed, and excluding various categories of people from warlike activities. As the basis for such legislation, biblical passages and principles were repeatedly quoted having to do with sexual behavior, war and peace, weekly rest, usury, and so on. Even so, throughout most of the Middle Ages, while the Bible was constantly repeated and studied in monasteries, convents, and cathedral chapters, this does not seem to have led to significant attempts to create a more just social order. The result was a highly hierarchical social order, both within the church and in society at large. This was partly justified on the basis of the writings of Pseudo-Dionysius, an unknown author who claimed to be Paul's disciple and whose writings were therefore given great authority until such claims were proven to be unfounded.

The Reformation of the sixteenth century brought with it profound changes in some of these matters, although not equally in every land and every theological tradition. In general, and with very significant exceptions, in Roman Catholic, Lutheran, and Anglican lands, the church was subjected to the state to such a degree that there were no great attempts at social change. Many among the Anabaptists did have a vision of a different social order, but the persecution to which they were subjected by almost all others limited their impact on society at large.

The theological tradition that most strenuously sought to shape a new social and political order on the basis of Scripture was the Reformed—that is, the tradition representing the views of Zwingli and Calvin. There were significant differences between Lutherans and the Reformed on the manner in which the Bible was to be interpreted, and therefore also on their attitudes vis-à-vis the social order. Disagreeing with Luther, Calvin insisted that the law has, besides its use in convicting us of sin and calling us to repentance, and in restraining evil, a "third use": leading believers not only in their personal lives but also in their social, political, and economic activities. This law of God must stand above any human law or order. This difference, which may not seem all that important, is one of the main reasons why, while the rest of Europe followed different paths, in the lands where the Reformed tradition developed deep roots—the Netherlands, Scotland, and, through the influence of the Puritans, England—there were soon revolutionary movements that sought to establish a social order more in agreement with the law of God.

It is interesting to note, however, that, with notable exceptions, most of these movements focused on what they considered doctrinal deviations (such as idolatry and "papism") or personal immoralities (such as debauchery and licentiousness), often leaving aside the emphasis of the ancient church on obedience to Scripture regarding the social and economic order.

3

THE INTERPRETATION OF THE BIBLE

CHAPTER 12

Models of Interpretation

All the first Christians, as well as Jesus himself, were Jews. Long before the advent of Christianity, the people of Israel already had very ancient books that they considered sacred. These were first of all the five books of the Law, or Torah, today commonly known as the "five books of Moses" or the Pentateuch. To these were added the "Prophets" and the books commonly known as the "Writings"—Psalms, Proverbs, etcetera. Although the limits of the Hebrew canon had not been defined by then, this would happen soon, and in any case the essential elements of the canon were already determined: the Law, the Prophets, and at least some of the Writings.

Also long before Christianity appeared on the scene, Jews had been interpreting their own Scripture. This may be seen not only in rabbinic writings about the Bible but also in the Bible itself, where we find authors rereading earlier books as they are challenged by new situations. Those who wrote during the exile and return to the Holy Land interpreted the entire story of the departure from Egypt in the light of what was taking place in their time. This may be seen in the book of Isaiah, among many other examples:

> Thus says the LORD,
>   who makes a way in the sea,
>   a passage in the mighty waters,
> who brings out chariot and horse,
>   army and warrior;
> they lie down, they cannot rise,
>   they are extinguished, quenched like a wick.
> . . . .
> I am about to do a new thing;
>   now it springs forth, do you not perceive it?
> I will make a way in the wilderness
>   and rivers in the desert.
>
> (Isa. 43:16–17, 19)

Later, when other Hebrew authors faced the oppression of the Hellenistic government in Syria, they read the histories of both the exodus and the exile as keys for understanding their own situation. In the first book of Maccabees, in a moment that could well have led to despair, Judas Maccabee extorts his followers:

> Do not fear their numbers or be afraid when they charge. Remember how our ancestors were saved at the Red Sea, when Pharaoh with his forces pursued them. And now, let us cry to Heaven, to see whether he will favor us and remember his covenant with our ancestors and crush this army before us today. Then all the Gentiles will know that there is one who redeems and saves Israel. (1 Macc. 4:8–11)

In summary, books in the Hebrew Bible provide us with interpretations of other books and passages in the Bible, applying them again and again to the various circumstances in which the Hebrew people found themselves.

Early Christians followed a similar pattern. Accepting the authority of the sacred books of the people of Israel, they would now read them from a different perspective. For them, the history of the liberation of Israel from the yoke of Egypt became an announcement of the liberation from the yoke of sin and death through Jesus Christ. Thus, just as the later books of the Old Testament reinterpret earlier ones, so does much of the New Testament reinterpret the Scriptures of Israel.

However, things were not all that easy. Most Jews did not accept such Christian reinterpretations. This gave rise to a polemic between Christians and Jews regarding the interpretation of the Hebrew Bible. Clearly, one of the main problems facing the earliest church was the matter of the relationship between the faith of Israel and the faith of Christians. The vast majority of Jews did not accept what Christians believed about Jesus and therefore saw in Christianity a rising heresy within the ranks of Israel. This may be seen as early as the book of Acts, where, taken before the Sanhedrin (the council of the Jews), Peter and John, and then Stephen, affirm that the death and resurrection of Jesus is the fulfillment of the promises found in the Scriptures of Israel. This in turn leads the leaders of Israel to flog Peter and John, and then to stone Stephen.

Convinced as they were that Jesus was the fulfillment of the promises made to Israel, those first Christians also considered themselves heirs to the Scriptures of Israel. As they saw matters, since Jesus was the Messiah who had been promised to Israel, Scripture pointed to him. Therefore, from its very first steps Christianity was compelled to reinterpret the Scriptures of Israel—and to do it usually in conflict with the majority of Jews, who would not accept the Christian interpretation, centering on Jesus as the Christ or Messiah. Again, the book of Acts attests to this. There Peter declares that what is taking place on the day of

Pentecost is the fulfillment of a prophecy of Joel's. Later, when the Sanhedrin asks him by what authority he has dared heal a lame man, Peter answers affirming that Jesus is the fulfillment of a prophecy to be found in Psalms:

> Let it be known to all of you, and to all the people of Israel, that this man is standing before you in good health by the name of Jesus Christ of Nazareth, whom you crucified, whom God raised from the dead. This Jesus is "the stone that was rejected by you, the builders; it has become the corner-stone." (Acts 4:10-11; cf. Ps. 118:22)

Later in the book of Acts, when Paul is beginning his missionary work in Antioch of Pisidia, he opens his statement by referring to the mighty acts of God in leading the people out of the land of Egypt "with uplifted arm" (Acts 13:17). As his speech progresses, he says of the leaders in Jerusalem that, by not recognizing Jesus or "understanding the words of the prophets that are read every sabbath, they fulfilled those words by condemning him" (Acts 13:27). In a word, Jesus himself is the fulfillment of the ancient prophecies.

These polemics between Christians and the Jews who had not accepted Jesus continued centering on the relationship between Jesus and the word of God expressed in Jewish Scriptures. We see this in the second century, among other writings, in Justin's *Dialogue with Trypho*. This is a rather extensive dialogue in which Justin records a conversation and debate with a Jew by the name of Trypho. Such a dialogue may have actually taken place, or it may be a literary composition by Justin himself based on what he had experienced in the polemics between Christians and Jews. At any rate, the dialogue shows a radical difference between the manner in which each of its two main participants interprets the Scriptures of Israel. Trypho simply cannot accept what Justin says, that the prophecies have been fulfilled in Jesus the Christ. Justin reads all the history of Israel as an announcement of Jesus himself. In this particular case, at the end of the dialogue, the two depart in relative friendship, and Justin ends by addressing Trypho and those who are with him as they prepare to board a ship: "I can wish no better thing for you, sirs, than this, that, recognising in this way that intelligence is given to every man, you may be of the same opinion as ourselves, and believe that Jesus is the Christ of God" (146.3; ANF 1:270).

This apparently friendly dialogue was not typical of what was taking place in other areas and circles. During the second half of the first century, the polemics became ever more bitter as the distance grew between those who accepted Jesus Christ and the more traditional Jews. In the late years of that century—that is, some fifty years before Justin's dialogue—Christians were officially expelled from the synagogue by Gamaliel II. After the temple had been destroyed, the Sanhedrin gathered in Jamnia under Gamaliel's leadership. It was there that the Hebrew canon was finally fixed. Apparently Gamaliel's decree was part of a wider effort to bring together all the Hebrew people and restore their faith after the destruction of the temple. It is also important to remember that at that point both Judaism and Christianity were seeking followers among the gentiles and were thus competing with one another in that regard. When Christianity became the dominant religion of the empire, and the only other religion that had a significant number of adherents was Judaism, several of the most famous Christian preachers sought to discredit Judaism, coming to the point of declaring that Jews were "deicides"—that is, murderers of God—and sometimes even inviting Christians to deal violently with them. It is a sad page in the history of Christianity that has often been forgotten and therefore has also been repeated.

There were also debates among those who called themselves followers of Christ. Most Christians affirmed the authority of the Scriptures of Israel. This was true even after the membership of the church ceased being mostly Jewish and became increasingly gentile. The Hebrew Scriptures are the word of God for the people of God, be it Israel or the church. There were, however, some Christians who simply rejected the Hebrew Scriptures, claiming that they had nothing to do with Christian faith and that the message of Jesus was completely alien to the faith of Israel. Most famous among those who held such opinions was Marcion, who lived in the second century.

Briefly stated, Marcion and his followers, rather than debating with Jews on the interpretation of the Scriptures of Israel, simply decided to leave aside those Scriptures, claiming that, although they were divinely revealed, the god who speaks there is not the same as the Father of Jesus Christ, but rather an inferior being. According to them, Israel's god is master and creator of the material world, while the true supreme God, the God whom Christians are to worship, is alien to the physical world and all material reality—including the human body. One of these two gods is just and requires payment, while the other, high above the first, is the God of love whose grace forgives. One of them created this material world, and the other reigns as a sovereign over purely spiritual reality. One of them wishes to have sacrifices offered and requires people to serve no other, while the other wishes that all spirits now imprisoned in the matter of body and earth will be able to escape from their captivity and rejoice with him.

Naturally, the disagreement between these two lines of interpretation went much further than the question of the authority of the Scriptures of Israel. For the church at large, its faith was the culmination of the faith of Israel, and the Christian God was the same as the God of Israel. For Marcion and those who followed his opinions, the two were quite disparate. This made an enormous difference in the way in which Jesus was to be understood. While most believers affirmed that Jesus was born of Mary and had a physical body just like any other human being, Marcion's followers denied all this, turning Jesus into a purely spiritual being who only seemed to be human—a view usually called "Docetism," after a Greek word meaning to seem or to appear.

Thus, with the traditional Jews on one side and Marcion and his followers (as well as Christian gnostics in general) on the other, most Christians felt compelled to affirm on the one hand the continuity between the God of Israel and their own God, and on the other that Jesus and Christian faith were the legitimate continuation and culmination of the faith of Israel, and the fulfillment of its Scriptures.

This was not easy, for the Hebrew Bible is a complex collection of different books representing a variety of genres and written in differing political and social circumstances. Within that diversity, the texts that could most easily be applied to Jesus were certain passages that were read as prophecies—in this case understanding prophecy not as the preaching or proclamation of a message given by God, but rather as an announcement of what would happen in the future.

This use of prophecy appears already in the most ancient Christian literature we have, which today we call the New Testament. There we find frequent references to certain passages of the Hebrew Bible that were understood as announcements about Jesus. One of the best known is found in Isaiah 53, which according to the book of Acts Philip interpreted to the Ethiopian eunuch as an announcement of the coming of Jesus and of his sufferings (Acts 8:32-35). Furthermore, we frequently find in the Gospels, particularly in Matthew, the notion that the ancient prophecies shape the very life of Jesus. Thus, for instance, when referring to the birth of Jesus, Matthew says that "all this took place to fulfill what had been spoken by the Lord through the prophet: 'Look, the virgin shall conceive and bear a son, and they shall name him Emmanuel'" (Matt. 1:22-23). Likewise,

Jesus and his family had to flee to Egypt so that a prophecy of Hosea could be fulfilled (Matt. 2:15).

Thus, much of the most ancient Christian interpretation of the Hebrew Bible consisted in seeking within that sacred text, whose authority Jews fully accepted, passages or words that could somehow be interpreted as announcements of the coming of Jesus and of various moments of his life and work. Apparently, soon someone collected lists of texts in the Old Testament that could be seen as prophecies about Jesus and that were therefore particularly useful in the polemics of Christians against Jews—the often called "books of testimonies." It is uncertain that such lists ever existed in written form, as actual documents circulating among Christians. Some scholars suggest that such documents did exist, while others believe that the list of testimonies was mostly a matter of an oral tradition circulating among believers. What is certain is that the same prophetic passages appear repeatedly in ancient Christian literature, frequently in a similar order, and this shows that there was a tradition—either written or oral—regarding passages of the Old Testament that could be understood as prophecies about Jesus.

It is clear, however, that such passages are only a minute portion of Hebrew Scripture, which includes not only prophecies but also laws, narratives, and several other literary genres. As to the laws, from an early time Christians began distinguishing between those whose purpose was to determine moral and social behavior and those that had different functions, particularly having to do with worship, sacrifices, ritual purity, and other similar matters. Ephesians, affirming that the gentiles and the children of Israel have come to be one, declares that Jesus "has abolished the law with its commandments and ordinances, that he might create in himself one new humanity in place of the two" (Eph. 2:15). Obviously, this did not refer to all the law, for commandments of a moral order were still in effect.

The process was not simple, particularly because the distinction between moral and ritual law is not always clear. Thus, in Acts 15, responding to the new conditions resulting from Paul's ministry among the gentiles, the church in Jerusalem notified gentile believers that, under the guidance of the Holy Spirit, it had decided "to impose on you no further burden than these essentials: that you abstain from what has been sacrificed to idols and from blood and from what is strangled and from fornication" (Acts 15:28-29). This indicates that for that early church in Jerusalem, dietetic laws having to do with the blood or eating animals that have not been blessed were part of the law that still had to be obeyed, jointly with others having to do with matters such as idolatry and sexual behavior. However, quite soon, as the church continued growing among gentiles, this residue of dietetic laws also came to be seen as part of the decrees that were no longer necessary to obey. Such was the case, for instance, regarding the meat of animals sacrificed to idols, about which Paul tells the Corinthians that the reason to abstain from such meat is not that eating it is evil in itself, but rather that it may be an occasion for the confusion of those who have less understanding and who, seeing others eating meat sacrificed to idols, may then fall into idolatry itself. This leads Paul to the conclusion that "if food is a cause of their falling, I will never eat meat, so that I may not cause one of them to fall" (1 Cor. 8:13).

Something similar occurred regarding the Sabbath—although among the requirements that the church in Jerusalem sets for gentile believers, the Sabbath itself is not mentioned. Early Christians, who were all Jews, continued keeping the Sabbath as a day of rest devoted to the Lord, while they also gathered on the first day of the week to break bread in memory, celebration, and anticipation of the resurrection of Jesus and his coming victory. (This is the reason why to this day, both in Greek and in most Romance languages, the last day of the week, which in English is called "Saturday," receives various names derived from "Sabbath.") But then, as the church made headway among gentiles, the keeping of the seventh day of the week as a day of rest became optative, as many gentile Christians were under a master, paterfamilias, or employer who would not allow them to take time off. Those who were able were encouraged to keep the Sabbath, while those who were not able were not required to do so. Eventually, as years and centuries went by, many of the original observances regarding the Sabbath were transferred to the first day of the week, Sunday.

However, distinguishing between ceremonial and moral law did not suffice, for the various laws having to do with ceremonies, diet, and the like are just as much a part of the Hebrew Bible as anything else, and Christians declared the entire Bible to be the word of God. How, then, could one declare such laws to be true and divine revelation, and still not follow them? Simply by understanding them as practices established by God so that they would point to Jesus Christ. As such, they had a very important function. But now that the event to which they pointed has already occurred, they have lost their validity as a commandment to obey and should be seen rather as signs or announcements of what God had always intended to do in Jesus. As a sign and announcement, their function is different once the reality they promised had come. One is no longer obliged to follow the sign, for its goal has been reached. But it is important still to remember the sign because it shows the purposes of God that are being fulfilled in history.

The ancient text that most clearly expresses this is in Justin's *Dialogue with Trypho*, which dates from the middle of the second century:

> For the Holy Spirit sometimes brought about that something, which was the type of the future, should be done clearly; sometimes He uttered words about what was to take

place, as if it was then taking place, or had taken place. And unless those who read perceive this art, they will not be able to follow the words of the prophets as they ought. For example's sake, I shall repeat some prophetic passages, that you may understand what I say. When He speaks by Isaiah, "He was led as a sheep to the slaughter, and like a lamb before the shearer," He speaks as if the suffering had already taken place. (114.1; *ANF* 1:256)

With these words Justin distinguishes between two sorts of announcements of Jesus in the Old Testament. The first is prophecy, which is well known, for it remains a favorite form of interpretation to this day. The most common case is the example that Justin himself gives, based on Isaiah 53.

The second sort of announcement of Jesus that we find in the Hebrew Scriptures are those that refer to him not in words about him, but rather in actions and events that were "types," "figures," or "shadows" of future events. Since the term Justin employs here is *typos*, this sort of interpretation is commonly called "typology." The theological foundation for typologies is the understanding that God acts following certain patterns that lead to and culminate in Jesus. Such typological interpretations appear already in the New Testament, almost a century before Justin. For instance, in 1 Corinthians 10, Paul speaks about the rock in the desert and claims that "the rock was Christ." Something similar may be seen in 1 Corinthians 5:7-8, where Paul tells his readers that "our paschal lamb, Christ, has been sacrificed."

The same sort of interpretation appears also in other ancient Christian literature. Although there are hundreds of such cases, a few examples will suffice to show how typological interpretation was applied. In Leviticus 12:3 it is ordered that every male child is to be circumcised on the eighth day after his birth. Explaining the significance of this law, Augustine says:

For good reason should an infant be baptized on the eighth day, because the stone with which we are circumcised was Christ. The Jewish people were circumcised with stone knives; but "the stone was Christ." Why on the eighth day? Because the first and the eighth days of the week are one and the same. After seven days, the first comes again. At the end of the seventh day the Lord was in the tomb, and he rose again when the first day returned, for his resurrection is for us a promise of life eternal, as is also the consecration of the first day of the week. (*Sermons* 169.3; BAC 53:180)

Another example of such typological reading of the Old Testament appears in Augustine's treatise on the Gospel of John—which is actually a collection of his sermons on that book. Here we find, besides several concrete examples, a further explanation of the manner in which the Scriptures of Israel speak to Christians typologically. Augustine says:

All things that were spoken to the ancient people Israel in the manifold Scripture of the holy law, what things they did, whether in sacrifices, or in priestly offices, or in feast-days, and, in a word, in what things soever they worshipped God, what things soever were spoken to and given them in precept, were shadows of things to come. Of what things to come? Things which find their fulfillment in Christ. Whence the apostle says, "For all the promises of God are in Him yea;" that is, they are fulfilled in Him. Again he says in another place, "All happened to them in a figure; but they were written for our sakes, upon whom the end of the ages is come." . . . If, therefore, all these things were shadows of things to come, also the feast of tabernacles was a shadow of things to come. Let us examine, then, of what thing to come was this feast-day a shadow. I have explained what this feast of tabernacles was: it was a celebration of tabernacles, because the people, after their deliverance from Egypt, while directing their course through the wilderness to the land of promise, dwelt in tents. Let us observe what it is, and we shall be that thing; we, I say, who are members of Christ, if such we are; but we are, He having made us worthy, not we having earned it for ourselves. Let us then consider ourselves, brethren: we have been led out of Egypt, where we were slaves to the devil as to Pharaoh; where we applied ourselves to works of clay, engaged in earthly desires, and where we toiled exceedingly. And to us, while laboring, as it were, at the bricks, Christ cried aloud, "Come unto me, all ye that labor and are heavy laden." Thence we were led out by baptism as through the Red Sea—red because consecrated by the blood of Christ. All our enemies that pursued us being dead, that is, all our sins being blotted out, we have been brought over to the other side. At the present time, then, before we come to the land of promise, namely, the eternal kingdom, we are in the wilderness in tabernacles. (*On the Gospel of John* 28.6; *NPNF*[1] 7:181–82)

Finally, it is important to point out that this sort of typological understanding is to be found in writers distant from one another in terms of both geography and theological perspectives. Consider, for instance, the words of Ephrem Syrus and Caesarius of Arles, one in the far reaches of the Eastern Roman Empire, and the other in the West, and therefore each already reflecting some of the differences that would eventually develop between Eastern and Western Christian theology. One may compare what these two say regarding the episode of the bronze serpent in the desert. Ephrem explains:

"Just as Moses lifted up the serpent in the desert, the Son of Man will be lifted up" [John 3:14]. Just as those who looked at the sign which Moses fastened on a pole lived bodily, so too, those who look with spiritual eyes at the body of the Messiah nailed and suspended on the cross, and believe in him, will live [spiritually]. Thus, it was revealed through this brazen [serpent], which by nature cannot suffer, that he who was to suffer on the cross is one who by nature cannot die. (*Commentary on the Diatessaron* 16.15; trans. Carmel McCarthy, Journal of Semitic Studies Supplement 2, 1993, p. 250)

Likewise, in one of his hymns he says:

Moses saw the uplifted serpent that had cured the bites of asps, and he looked to see Him who would heal the ancient Serpent's wound. Moses saw that he himself alone retained the brightness from God, and he looked for Him who came. (*Hymns on the Nativity* 1; NPNF² 13:224)

And, at the other extreme of the Mediterranean world, Caesarius declares:

Although this serpent seems to be quite wonderful, dearly beloved, still it prefigured the Incarnation of the Lord. Perhaps this thought might seem difficult to some men, if the Lord Himself had not spoken in the Gospel. Thus He said: "As Moses lifted up the serpent in the desert, even so must the Son of Man be lifted up." That brazen serpent was then hung on a pole, because Christ was to be hung on the cross. At that time whoever had been struck by a serpent looked on the brazen serpent and was healed. Now the human race which was struck by the spiritual serpent, the devil, looks upon Christ with faith and is healed. If a man had been struck and failed

to behold that brazen serpent, he died. So it is, brethren: if
a man does not believe in Christ crucified, he is slain by the
poison of the devil. Then, a man looked at the dead serpent
in order to escape the live one; now, if a man wants to avoid
the devil's poison, he looks on Christ crucified. (*Sermons*
112.1; FC 2:151–52)

Such typological interpretation was applied not only to ritual, dietetic, and purity laws but also to the entire history of
Israel. In ancient Christian literature, the exodus is repeatedly
presented as a type or figure of the work of Jesus in freeing souls
from hell. The ark of Noah in which he and his family as well
the animals are saved in the midst of the waters of the flood is a
foreshadowing of baptism. The manna that fed the people in the
desert announced the bread of life, Jesus Christ, as well as the
bread of Communion. The many sterile women who gave birth
to great leaders in the history of Israel were an announcement
of Mary who, being a virgin and therefore the sterile woman par
excellence, gave birth to Jesus. And so forth.

Typological interpretation does not deny the historical reality of the narratives in the Old Testament. On the contrary, it
takes for granted that such events did indeed take place, while
asserting that they also had a further meaning pointing to the
future. In reading Scripture as an announcement of the future,
typology is often confused with prophecy, and therefore there
are numerous cases in which what we find in the New Testament or in other Christian writings may be interpreted as either
prophecy or typology—from which different readings result. For
instance, it is common to read Isaiah 53 as prophecy. This means
that when the prophet spoke these words, he was not referring in
any way to what was happening in his time, but rather announcing what would take place years later in the passion of Jesus. If,
on the other hand, we understand Isaiah 53 typologically, we

will believe that the prophet was referring to something that was taking place in his time, and we may even try to discover what this was. But we would still see what was happening then as an announcement or a sign of things to come. Furthermore, there are also ancient Christian writers who project typology beyond the time of its fulfillment in Jesus, applying it to the life of the church and believers. When Isaiah 53 is thus interpreted, the passage refers not only to what happened in the life of Jesus and in previous instances in the history of Israel, but also to the manner in which Christians are to live following the pattern of the suffering servant. This use of the passage may be seen in the First Epistle of Peter, who, while instructing slaves not to respond with violence and hatred to a possible abuse on the part of their masters but rather to show a patience similar to that of the suffering servant, tells them:

> If you endure when you are beaten for doing wrong, what credit is that? But if you endure when you do right and suffer for it, you have God's approval. For to this you have been called, because Christ also suffered for you, leaving you an example, so that you should follow in his steps. "He committed no sin, and no deceit was found in his mouth." When he was abused, he did not return abuse; when he suffered, he did not threaten; but he entrusted himself to the one who judges justly. He himself bore our sins in his body on the cross, so that, free from sins, we might live for righteousness; by his wounds you have been healed. For you were going astray like sheep, but now have returned to the Shepherd and guardian of your souls. (1 Pet. 2:20-25)

Therefore, as we now read the many references in the New Testament to the prophecies of Israel, it may be helpful to consider the possibility that such references may also have a typological dimension. For instance, there is in 1 Peter another passage in which a typology is projected forward into the life of the church. This is a reference to Jesus as the stone that was cast out by the builders and that has now become the cornerstone of the entire building, which the epistle then uses to call its readers to become themselves as living stones in the great building or spiritual house that God is constructing:

> Come to him, a living stone, though rejected by mortals yet chosen and precious in God's sight, and like living stones, let yourselves be built into a spiritual house, to be a holy priesthood, to offer spiritual sacrifices acceptable to God through Jesus Christ. For it stands in scripture: "See, I am laying in Zion a stone, a cornerstone chosen and precious; and whoever believes in him will not be put to shame." To you then who believe, he is precious; but for those who do not believe, "The stone that the builders rejected has become the very head of the corner," and "A stone that makes them stumble, and a rock that makes them fall." (1 Pet. 2:4-8)

Finally, besides prophetic and typological interpretations, we also find in the ancient church frequent allegorical readings. In such interpretations the literal and historical sense of a text is eclipsed by its symbolic meaning. Allegory had become a common method by which the pagan Hellenistic world interpreted its own ancient texts. In that world, the writings of authors such as Homer and Hesiod were the basic textbooks used by educators to help shape their students' lives and values. However, most of the myths about the gods that were told in those classical writings had lost prestige and credibility during the Hellenistic period. Therefore, when reading such classical authors, the purpose was not so much to understand the literal words about the various myths, but rather to find in those stories symbolic and deeper meanings regarding moral and civil life. Surrounded by this practice, which was considered quite proper, Christians too came to interpret the Scriptures of Israel allegorically.

Allegory has remained a common method of biblical interpretation throughout history. In the ancient church, those who led the way into this sort of interpretation were Clement of Alexandria and above all his disciple Origen. According to them, every text has at least two meanings—and in some cases, several more. One of the basic meanings of a text is its literal sense. The other, much higher than the first, is what they called the "spiritual" meaning—that is, the allegorical meaning. With a certain measure of intellectual elitism, they claimed that the literal meaning was for the unlearned, while the spiritual was to be discovered by those who had a deeper understanding. When one finds a literal meaning that seems to contradict the teaching of the rest of Scripture, that literal meaning must be completely abandoned in favor of a spiritual interpretation. Origen claimed that much of the "error" of the Jews was that they let themselves be carried by literal interpretations of passages that in truth were "spiritual" or allegorical. A typical case is the manner in which he deals with the taking and destruction of the city of Ai in Joshua 8:

> When the Jews read these things they become cruel and thirst after human blood, thinking that even holy persons so struck those who were living in Ai that not one of them was left "who might be saved or who might escape." They do not understand that mysteries are dimly shadowed in the words and that they more truly indicate to us that we ought not to leave any of these demons deeply within, . . . but to destroy them all. (*Homilies on Joshua* 8.7; FC 105:92)

This form of interpretation was particularly attractive at a time when Christians were accused of being ignorant and giving great credence and esteem to books that spoke of harsh crimes and terrible revenge. Responding to such claims, people such as Origen could offer interpretations of the biblical text that employed a method similar to what the cultured pagans did when reading Homer and the other classical authors. A case in point is Augustine, who was not ready to accept the faith of his mother, Monica, because the stories he read in Scripture seemed to him coarse and violent. It was upon hearing the preaching of Ambrose, who frequently interpreted the most difficult passages allegorically, that Augustine could finally accept the authority of Scripture.

However, while allegorical interpretation makes it possible to say something apparently significant about any biblical passage, it has the enormous disadvantage of allowing the interpreter to determine what the text says—which actually takes authority away from the text and gives it to the interpreter. Origen himself developed an entire system of hidden meanings connected with certain words in the Bible, so that he understood "cloud" to mean "voice," for example, and "horse" indicated "strength." This he did to such a point that a scholar has correctly declared that in Origen the Bible has become not so much a divine revelation as a divine puzzle whose solution only Origen can find.

It did not take modern scholars to criticize the exaggerations of allegorism. In the fourth century, Basil the Great spoke quite clearly about this:

> I know the laws of allegory, though less by myself than from the works of others. There are those truly, who do not admit the common sense of the Scriptures, for whom water is not water, but some other nature, who see in a plant, in a fish, what their fancy wishes, who change the nature of reptiles and of wild beasts to suit their allegories, like the interpreters of dreams who explain visions in sleep to make them

serve their own ends. For me grass is grass; plant, fish, wild beast, domestic animal, I take all in the literal sense. (*Hexameron* 9.1; *NPNF*² 8:101)

Having considered these various models of interpretation, it is important to point out that, although there are marked differences among these models, in the writings of any of the ancient Christian authors one may find examples of all three, even though each author will show a preference for one of them. Furthermore, even though the three approaches mentioned here seem to be the main models of interpretation, among the ancients there were many others. In a document written in 393, Augustine lists four different ways of understanding Genesis—to which it would be necessary to add prophecy, which he does not mention. He says:

> Various writers expound the Law in four different ways. These may be given Greek names, and then explained in Latin, as "history, allegory, analogy, and etiology." We interpret matters historically when we narrate events, be they human or divine; allegorically, when events and words are taken figuratively; analogically, when the agreement between the Old Testament and the New is made clear; and etiologically, when the causes and reasons for such events and words are offered. (*On the Literal Interpretation of Genesis* [incomplete] 2.5; BAC 168:502–4)

Looking, then, in a more general way at the entire corpus of ancient Christian literature, there is no doubt that for a sizable number of authors, typology—or "analogy," as Augustine called it—was the preferred method for relating the Hebrew Bible to the gospel of Jesus and to the life of the church. The entire Hebrew Bible is then understood as putting forth patterns in the action of God in which Christians have a place. Some of those patterns are laws that should guide all human behavior, and others are a foreshadowing of what would be fulfilled in Jesus.

Finally, on this issue of examining Scripture in order to find its hidden meanings or answers to all our questions, the advice Irenaeus offered around the year 190 is still valid for the twenty-first century:

> If, therefore, even with respect to creation, there are some things [the knowledge of] which belongs only to God, and others which come within the range of our own knowledge, what ground is there for complaint, if, in regard to those things which we investigate in the Scriptures (which are throughout spiritual), we are able by the grace of God to explain some of them, while we must leave others in the hands of God, and that not only in the present world, but also in that which is to come, so that God should for ever teach, and man should for ever learn the things taught him by God? . . . Because He is good, and possesses boundless riches, a kingdom without end, and instruction that can never be exhausted. (*Against Heresies* 2.28.3; ANF 1:399-400)

CHAPTER 13

Crucial Texts: Creation

The very first words of the Bible refer to creation. To affirm the doctrine of creation is to say at once something unique about God and something unique about the whole created universe. As to the first, Scripture repeatedly contrasts the true God, maker of all things, with idols, which are made by humans (Isa. 49:9-20; Hos. 8:4b). But the same Scripture also makes it clear that the God who at the beginning made heaven and earth is constantly doing new things. The verb "to create" in its strictest sense can be applied only to these actions of God—actions such as the creation of the people of Israel and the creation at the end of history of a new heaven and new earth. Therefore, when speaking of God as creator, we should not limit our view to the very first action by which God created heaven and earth. The creator God of Genesis 1 and 2 is still the creator God, always creating.

Furthermore, creation does not appear only in Genesis, but rather is a theme that emerges again and again throughout Scripture. The psalmist refers to the greatness of creation in contrast to the smallness of the human beings within it: "When I look at your heavens, the work of your fingers, the moon and the stars that you have established; what are human beings that you are mindful of them, mortals that you care for them?" (Ps. 8:3-4). Likewise, the prophets refer to the greatness of creation as a call to justice: "Ah, you that turn justice to wormwood, and bring righteousness to the ground! The one who made the Pleiades and Orion, and turns deep darkness into the morning, and darkens the day into night, who calls for the waters of the sea, and pours them out on the surface of the earth, the LORD is his name" (Amos 5:7-8).

From the ancient Israelites Christianity learned and inherited the doctrine of creation. The Fourth Gospel places creation at the very beginning of what it has to say about Jesus: "In the beginning was the Word, and the Word was with God, and the Word was God. He was in the beginning with God. All things came into being through him, and without him not one thing came into being. . . . And the Word became flesh . . ." (John 1:1-3, 14).

This doctrine is paramount not only in Scripture but also in early Christian literature. Both the Didache (1.2) and the so-called Epistle of Barnabas (10.2) include the commandment "You shall love him who has made you." In the First Epistle of Clement to the Corinthians, written late in the first century, the doctrine of creation is strongly affirmed and then employed to exhort the Corinthian Christians to follow a harmony similar to that which God has stamped on the universe:

> Wherefore, having so many great and glorious examples set before us, let us turn again to the practice of that peace which from the beginning was the mark set before us; and let us look stedfastly to the Father and Creator of the universe, and cleave to His mighty and surpassingly great gifts and benefactions of peace. Let us contemplate Him with our understanding, and look with the eyes of our soul to His long-suffering will. Let us reflect how free from wrath He is towards all His creation.

The heavens, revolving under His government, are subject to Him in peace. Day and night run the course appointed by Him, in no wise hindering each other. The sun and moon, with the companies of the stars, roll on in harmony according to His command, within their prescribed limits, and without any deviation. The fruitful earth, according to His will, brings forth food in abundance, at the proper seasons, for man and beast and all the living beings upon it, never hesitating, nor changing any of the ordinances which He has fixed. The unsearchable places of abysses, and the indescribable arrangements of the lower world, are restrained by the same laws. The vast unmeasurable sea, gathered together by His working into various basins, never passes beyond the bounds placed around it, but does as He has commanded. For He said, "Thus far shalt thou come, and thy waves shall be broken within thee." The ocean, impassible to man, and the worlds beyond it, are regulated by the same enactments of the Lord. The seasons of spring, summer, autumn, and winter, peacefully give place to one another. The winds in their several quarters fulfil, at the proper time, their service without hindrance. The ever-flowing fountains, formed both for enjoyment and health, furnish without fail their breasts for the life of men. The very smallest of living beings meet together in peace and concord. All these the great Creator and Lord of all has appointed to exist in peace and harmony; while He does good to all, but most abundantly to us who have fled for refuge to His compassions through Jesus Christ our Lord, to whom be glory and majesty for ever and ever. (19–20; *ANF* 1:10-11)

Several centuries later, Athanasius of Alexandria would marvel,

Who that sees the circle of heaven and the course of the sun
and the moon, and the positions and movements of the other
stars, as they take place in opposite and different directions,
while yet in their difference all with one accord observe a
consistent order, can resist the conclusion that these are not
ordered by themselves, but have a maker distinct from themselves who orders them? Or who that sees the sun rising by
day and the moon shining by night, and waning and waxing
without variation exactly according to the same number of
days, and some of the stars running their courses and with
orbits various and manifold, while others move without
wandering, can fail to perceive that they certainly have a creator to guide them? (*Against the Gentiles* 3.35.4; NPNF² 4:23)

As Christianity made its way into Greco-Roman culture, it
had to confront a vast variety of opinions regarding the universe.
The ancient myths about the pagan gods and their connection
with nature had lost much of their power, but polytheism was
still rampant among the public at large. Among the more educated elite, there were different views regarding the nature of
the universe. According to Epicurus and Epictetus, all that exists
is matter, made up of atoms. What we call "spirit" is simply a
more subtle matter, made up of smaller atoms. Among others
who followed the teachings of Stoicism, there was a sort of pan-
theism that tended to regard all existence as somehow divine.
The Platonism of the time, which was evolving to become what
today we call Neoplatonism, proposed theories of emanation
according to which all that exists is a series of emanations or
waves derived from the Ineffable One. The further away any reality stands from that original One, the more material it is and
therefore the less valuable. Besides these various philosophical
theories, there was also a great variety of gnostic schools that,

while differing on many other points, in general agreed on a negative view of matter—a view based on a radical dualism in which all that is spiritual is good and all that is material is evil.

From an early date there were those who sought to join the message and person of Jesus with a view of reality as a mixture of an evil matter and a spiritual good. This was particularly true of gnostic teachers who sought to co-opt Jesus into their doctrinal systems, turning him into a sort of phantom or appearance with no material reality. However, the outstanding figure supporting this radical dichotomy between matter and spirit was not a gnostic but the son of a Christian bishop whose name was Marcion, whom we have already met. Being the son of a bishop, Marcion knew the Scriptures of Israel and even took them to be divine revelation. His conviction that the god revealed in the Hebrew Bible is a different and lesser god than the God and Father of Jesus Christ implied a denial not only of creation but also of the incarnation, the resurrection, and all judgment.

By the middle of the second century, the church was deeply concerned about such teachings, which it saw as a threat to the very heart of the gospel. This is why we read in 1 John 4:2–3 that "every spirit that confesses that Jesus Christ has come in the flesh is from God, and every spirit that does not confess Jesus is not from God." The antichrist mentioned after these words is not defined in terms of its moral evil, nor is it presented as persecuting Christians, but rather is defined by its Docetism. The clear opposition of these words of 1 John—as well as other passages in the same epistle—to any form of Docetism gave rise to an ancient tradition regarding John and Cerinthus, one of the main teachers of gnostic Docetism. According to this tradition, which may well have evolved out of this passage in 1 John, when Cerinthus came across John in the city of Ephesus, Cerinthus asked John, "Do you know me?" To which John responded, "Yes, I know you, son of Satan."

Furthermore, what we now call the Apostles' Creed began to take shape in the second century, mostly in order to make it very clear that the teachings of Marcion were not acceptable. Ancient creeds were baptismal formulae, frequently presented in an interrogative format to a person about to be baptized. That person was asked, for instance, "Do you believe in God the Father Almighty?" To which the person was expected to answer, "Yes, I believe." This is why ancient creeds have a Trinitarian structure, reflecting baptism in the name of the Father, the Son, and the Holy Spirit. Such creeds were then also used as a means for mutual recognition among believers, in order to make sure that someone affirmed the faith of the church. Because these ancient creeds were being formed in the second century, when Marcion and his doctrines seemed to be a great threat, they all have an anti-Marcionite character, with a strong emphasis on creation and on the incarnation of God in Jesus Christ.

The teachings of Marcion were also one of the main challenges leading to the formation of the canon of the New Testament—a canon that strongly asserts the continuity between the two testaments by constantly quoting passages from the Hebrew Bible.

It was partly in reaction to the opinions of Marcion and others like him that the great teachers of early Christianity emphasized the doctrine of creation. Obviously, this led them to pay great attention to the first chapters of Genesis, where the entire creation is declared to be good. Something similar continues throughout the history of Christian literature, beginning, as we have seen, with the oldest books we have outside the New Testament—documents such as the epistles of Clement of Rome and Ignatius of Antioch.

But, while most who claimed the name "Christian" affirmed the doctrine of creation, not all understood it in the same way. In general, as soon as more extensive literature appeared within the church—mostly late in the second century and early in the third—there were three basic ways of looking at creation. One of these simply saw creation as the beginning of all things. This is how most believers today understand the doctrine of creation. From such a perspective, creation was something that happened a long time ago, resulting in the existence of the world. Once the sixth day of creation was reached in the Genesis story, creation was complete and was exactly what God wished it to be forever. Had it not been for the intervention of the serpent and of sin with it, all would have remained as it was then. When one sees creation in this manner, the normal result is that all human history becomes a process whose main purpose is simply to restore the lost perfection. In the literature we have from those early centuries, the main exponent of this understanding of creation—an understanding that has become common throughout Western theology, both Catholic and Protestant—was Tertullian, who lived in North Africa late in the second century and early in the third.

Another way to understand creation that was proposed in the ancient church, but that generally did not receive great credence, is based on the existence of two parallel stories of creation in the early chapters of Genesis. One of these includes the entire first chapter of Genesis and the early verses of the next chapter. At that point the second narrative begins, covering most of the second chapter of the book. This duality of stories of creation, which may surprise some people today and which is often thought to be a fairly modern discovery—perhaps the product of people who do not believe in Scripture—was well known in antiquity by biblical scholars, Jewish as well as Christian. In the first story, everything revolves around the six days of creation. Here God begins by creating everything else, including the animals, and finally the human being, both male and female. In the other story, God begins by creating the man, then the garden where God places the man next to the animals (which do not quite serve as company to the man), and finally the woman, who is formed out of the rib of the man and is therefore a fit companion to him. How are these parallel but different stories to be coordinated? It was in response to this question that a particular way of understanding creation arose, first among Jewish scholars, and then among Christians—particularly with Origen, early in the third century. Origen read both stories literally and therefore reached the conclusion that there were in fact two creations, or two stages in creation. At first, God created only spiritual beings. This is the creation described in Genesis 1. When these spiritual beings—or rather, some of them—ceased contemplating God, they fell. God then made the material creation as a temporary abode for these fallen spirits until they were able to return to their pure spirituality. This is the creation to which Genesis 2 refers. According to this view, eventually all the fallen spirits will return to their spiritual origin, and the material world will disappear. As was to be expected, such an interpretation was not well received among most believers and was soon abandoned, and even declared heretical. Even so, the views of Origen and others like him persisted in the notion, widespread among believers, that God really loves and is concerned only for spiritual creation, and that all that is material is second rate.

This tendency to value the spiritual above the material, and sometimes even to consider the material to be evil, has repeatedly appeared throughout the history of Christianity. A distinguished theologian who contributed to this in some measure was Augustine, who had been a Neoplatonist before his conversion and whose Christian writings, particularly early on, contain vestiges of this philosophy. But the one who really made this understanding prevalent throughout the Middle Ages was an unknown author who, late in the fifth century or early in the sixth, wrote a series of works claiming he was Dionysius, the man whom Paul converted at the Areopagus (Acts 17:34). This Pseudo-Dionysius proposed a form of mysticism deeply influenced by Platonism and in which everything was seen as a hierarchy that made the material inferior to the spiritual. Since by passing as a disciple of Paul he enjoyed almost apostolic authority, Pseudo-Dionysius left a profound imprint on medieval thought. His teachings also served to bolster the highly hierarchical ordering of medieval society.

A third understanding of creation was fairly common in the ancient church but was eventually set aside or forgotten by most Western theologians. This understanding reads the stories of Genesis not as the entire history of creation, but rather as the account of its beginning. The main ancient author who clearly held such a perspective is Irenaeus, bishop of Lyons, in the late second century. In referring to the narratives in Genesis, rather than calling them "the creation," he repeatedly calls them "the beginning of creation." The constant repetition of this phrase makes it clear that he is purposefully trying to affirm that God's creative work is still continuing. The Creator continues creating. Certainly, the creation of which Genesis speaks was good; but it was not complete. Irenaeus expresses this by saying that humans were "as children," and that they were to "grow in justice and knowledge of the word of God" (*Demonstration of the Apostolic Preaching* 12). This implies that their perfection consisted not in having reached their goal but in being what they were intended to be at that particular moment of the creative process. God's purpose was that creation would continue progressing toward the goal of the new creation to which Revelation refers. Sin broke into that process, and therefore what should have been a history of continuous growth toward the fulfillment of God's designs was twisted and misshapen. God continued working to bring all of creation to its final purpose, creating the people of Israel, giving them the law, coming in Jesus Christ, creating the church and giving it the Holy Spirit—all leading to its culmination in the new heaven and new earth promised in Revelation. Within the context of this understanding of creation, part of God's plan is that what began in a garden would lead to a city. In other words, the history of humankind and its process of civilization, even though twisted by sin, is part of God's plan.

Even while these different interpretations—and their more modern counterparts—have long existed, the doctrine of creation has always been a pillar of Christian faith, a pillar that has been repeatedly attacked by others, including philosophers, poets, and scientists. Most of these attacks are not directed at the very notion of a divine creative action, but rather at some of the elements of the Genesis narratives. More recently, there has been a long-standing confrontation between those who insist that all things were made in six days and those who affirm that species have evolved. Among the first, what is often defended is not the biblical narratives as they appear in the sacred text, but rather a somewhat arbitrary selection and joining of elements taken from both narratives in Genesis and an ignoring of those others that do not fit into the proposed scheme. Among the second group, though, those who absolutely reject any notion of purposeful creation on a supposedly scientific basis go beyond the limits of science, which can never prove their assertions.

Such debates are not new. In a way, they are similar to those that arose when it was suggested that it is not the sun that revolves around the earth, but vice versa. When the Copernican system was first proposed, many church leaders declared that such a thing could not be true, for it contradicted the affirmation in Joshua 10 that the sun and the moon stood still. Much earlier there were already similar conflicts, as may be seen in Augustine's rejection of those who try to hide their ignorance by claiming that their views are biblical. Augustine sees such claims not as mere errors but as grave dangers and a threat to

Christian faith, making it seem what it is not and thereby putting many souls at risk. He says:

> It often happens that a non-believer knows by means of reason and of experience a number of things of earth, of the sky, and of the rest of this world. He knows the movements, rotation, size and distance of heavenly bodies. He knows about eclipses of the Sun and of the Moon, of the cycles of years and of time, of the nature of animals, of fruits, stones and other similar things. In such a case, it is shameful and damaging, and most to be avoided, for a Christian to speak of these things claiming to base his opinions on Scripture, for when the non-believer hears such vagaries he cannot but laugh at them. The resulting evil is not in such laughter, but rather in non-believers coming to the conclusion that our sacred authors actually defend such errors. As a result, as we work for the health of their souls, they judge us to be ignorant, and treat us as such, to the great detriment of their souls. When those who do not believe know something perfectly well, and find Christians to be in error and affirming that what they say is based on the divine books, how are they to believe what our books say about the resurrection of the dead, and the hope of eternal life, and the kingdom of heaven? They will decide that our books err, for their own experience and thinking show that what Christians say is not true. When such Christians, in order to defend what they said without sufficient thought and obvious error, try to support their statements on the divine books, or quote them by heart hoping to prove their point, they throw words to the wind, for they understand not what they say. These daring and presumptuous people cause unmeasurable sadness and annoyance to the more prudent brothers when they are refuted by

those who attribute no authority to the divine books. (*A Literal Commentary on Genesis* 1.19.39; BAC 168:614–16)

More than a millennium after Augustine, in the sixteenth century, John Calvin faced a similar question. Astronomers were beginning to discover that there are many stars and planets that are much larger than the moon. Does Scripture then err? Calvin's response may be helpful today as believers seek to deal with apparent conflicts between science and faith:

The Holy Spirit had no intention to teach astronomy; and, in proposing instruction meant to be common to the simplest and most uneducated persons, he made use by Moses and the other Prophets of popular language, that none might shelter himself under the pretext of obscurity, as we will see men sometimes very readily pretend an incapacity to understand, when anything deep or recondite is submitted to their notice. (*Commentary on Psalms* 136.7, in *Calvin's Commentaries*, vol. 6 [Grand Rapids: Baker Book House, 1979], 184–85)

In any case, by focusing attention on creation as only the beginning of all things and on how the biblical narrative differs from scientific explanations, we have often missed other important dimensions and consequences of the creation of all things by God.

First, we need to remember that creation is not only about God but also about that which God creates. Even a cursory reading of Genesis 1, with its repetitive theme that "God saw that it was good," should lead us to the conclusion that all creation—all that exists—is good. In this affirmation, it is crucial to emphasize the word "all." Along these lines, biblical scholars, as well as students of ancient tongues and their idioms, tell us that when

Genesis speaks of "heavens" and "earth," it is not referring to two specific places, or to two realms beyond which there may be others. The phrase "heavens and earth" means absolutely every-thing—just as when we say "kit and caboodle" we are not saying that "kit" is some things, "caboodle" is some others, and then there may still be others not included. What Genesis means is that God made the whole thing, kit and caboodle! This is stated, among others, by Basil the Great, who says, "By naming the two extremes, he suggests the substance of the whole world, accord-ing to heaven the privilege of seniority, and putting earth in the second rank. All intermediate beings were created at the same time as the extremities" (*Hexameron* 1.7; *NPNF*[2] 8:56).

The goodness of creation is a fundamental tenet of both Ju-daism and Christianity. All that God has made—and therefore all that exists—is good. This obviously leads to the question of the existence of evil. If all is good, how do we explain a virus that kills millions of people? Through the ages, theologians and philosophers have proposed numerous solutions to this puzzle—none of them satisfactory. Clearly, evil is, at least in part, the result of sin. But the question still remains, why does God allow sin? Perhaps all we can say is that evil is a great mystery—the "mystery of iniquity"—and that it is precisely our inability to explain it away that makes it truly evil.

Second, the doctrine of creation also means that there is an order in the universe. In the Apostles' Creed, the Greek word that we usually translate as "almighty" or "omnipotent" is *panto-crator*. This word is derived from two roots, one meaning "all"—as in *pan*demic or *pan*theism—and the other "government" or "rule"—as in demo*cracy* or merito*cracy*. Thus, when we say that God, "maker of heaven and earth," is "almighty," what we are affirming is not primarily that God can do whatever God desires, but rather that *all* that exists is under the rule or *government* of God. Obviously, this does not mean there is no such thing as sin and evil. But it does mean there is an order in all things.

Without such a notion of an all-encompassing order, modern science would be impossible. Today, after many centuries of scientific development, it may be difficult for us to realize the enormous significance for the course of human history of monotheism and its connection with the notion of an established natural order. In a polytheistic world, whatever happens is explained by the whims of the gods and conflicts among them. If it rains, it is because at present the god of rain prevails over the god of sunshine; and if the sun shines, it is for the opposite reason. In contrast, in a world created by an all-ruling God, there is an order; and, since our minds are part of that creation, there must be some correlation between the order in our minds and the order in the world—thus making the world at least partly understandable. So although today many think there is an insurmountable breach between science and the doctrine of creation, in truth the monotheism required by the doctrine of creation stands at the very root of the notion of science itself.

Third, while the doctrine of creation insists on the goodness of all that exists, it also makes it clear that not one of these things—nor all of them together—is God. What exists is not an emanation from the Divine. When God creates, God produces another reality that is not God. Although the creatures may point to their Creator, there is an unbreachable gap between creation and Creator. This must be stressed at a time when the most common form of idolatry is precisely overvaluing created things as if they were divine.

Finally, Christian reflection on creation soon led theologians to affirm that God makes the universe out of nothing—*ex nihilo*. This is not to be seen as a description of what existed before creation—"nothing," which after all is too abstract for our minds to grasp. It is rather another way of saying that everything owes its existence to God, and that therefore things, even though good, are not to be taken as the ultimate reality. Basil of Caesarea expressed this as follows: "If matter is uncreated, it has a claim to the same honours as God, since it must be of equal rank with Him. Is this not the summit of wickedness, that an extreme deformity, without quality, without form, shape, ugliness without configuration, to use their own expression, should enjoy the same prerogatives with Him, Who is wisdom, power and beauty itself?" (*Hexameron* 2.2; *NPNF*[2] 8:59).

CHAPTER 14

Crucial Texts: The Exodus

W hen we read through the Old Testament, it becomes evident that the story of the exodus is at the very heart of Hebrew faith. From a traditional Jewish perspective, the great saving act of God that sets the pattern for all other divine interventions throughout history is the deliverance of Israel from the yoke of Egypt. The psalmist praises the faithfulness of God by reminding Israel that God "divided the sea and let them pass through it, and made the waters stand like a heap. In the daytime he led them with a cloud, and all night long with a fiery light. He split rocks open in the wilderness, and gave them drink abundantly as from the deep" (Ps. 78:13-16). Similar declarations may be found throughout the Psalms—see, for instance, Psalms 80, 105, 106, 135, and 136. These songs celebrate the history of divine deliverance from Egypt and divine care through the desert. The exodus story marked—and still marks—the identity of the people of Israel.

When the people are in exile and longing to return to their homeland, Isaiah reminds them of the great interventions of God in the exodus, and he reminds them of that story by asking, "Where is the one who put within them [the people] his holy spirit, who caused his glorious arm to march at the right hand of Moses, who divided the waters before them to make for himself an everlasting name, who led them through the depths?" (Isa. 63:11b–13a). Now this same God, through a voice crying out in the wilderness, promises to make a highway in the desert just as before a path was opened across the sea.

This typological view of the exodus was carried on into Christianity from New Testament times. John the Baptist is seen as a voice crying out in the wilderness—which does not mean, as that phrase is commonly understood, that no one will listen, but rather that, like Isaiah, John is announcing the highway to liberation that God is about to open (John 1:23). Jesus is "the Lamb of God who takes away the sin of the world" (John 1:29), just as the blood of the Passover lamb saved the firstborns of Israel. As the Lamb of God, Jesus is sacrificed at Passover. Following the pattern of Moses, who freed Israel from the yoke of Egypt, Jesus through his resurrection frees his followers from the yoke of sin and death. This is why Paul can declare that "our paschal lamb, Christ, has been sacrificed" (1 Cor. 5:7). Numerous typological interpretations are then joined to this: just as Israel was forty years in the desert, Jesus too was forty days in the desert; just as the children of Israel were saved by crossing the waters of the sea, so too must the followers of Jesus go through the waters of baptism; just as the serpent was raised in the desert, so too was Jesus raised on the cross; just as God called Israel out of Egypt, so too did God call Jesus out of Egypt; and it is clear that the plagues and calamities described in the book of Revelation follow the pattern of the plagues in Egypt.

Following what they had learned from Israel, early Christians interpreted their own faith as the fulfillment of what had been announced typologically from the time of the exodus and throughout the history of Israel. This gave shape not only to biblical interpretation but also to Christian worship.

Even a rapid reading of the most outstanding Christian leaders of antiquity shows the prevalence of this typological reading
of the exodus story. Commenting on Exodus 2:10, which deals
with the infancy of Moses, Caesarius of Arles says:

> If we notice carefully, dearly beloved, we realize that just like
> blessed Isaac, Joseph, and Jacob, so also Moses represented
> a type of Christ. Moreover, consider still more attentively
> and you will see what great mysteries were prefigured in
> him. Moses was born of a Jewish woman and adopted by
> the daughter of Pharaoh. Now Pharaoh's daughter prefig-
> ured the Church because she left the house of her father and
> came to wash herself in the water. Pharaoh is accepted as a
> type of the devil; his daughter, as I said, is understood as the
> Church. . . . Thus God the Father admonishes her that she
> should leave her father, the devil. For this reason this Church
> which left the house of her father, the devil, and hastened to
> the water, that is, to the waters of Baptism, to be washed of
> the sins which she had contracted in the house of her father.
> (*Sermons* 95.1; FC 47:65)

Earlier, late in the second century, Irenaeus had affirmed that
in the last analysis the one who gave the law on Mount Sinai was
not Moses but Christ himself. Interpreting the story of Moses in
the light of Romans 10:4, where Paul declares that "Christ is the
end of the law," Irenaeus comments:

> And how is Christ the end of the law, if He be not also the
> final cause of it? For He who has brought in the end has
> Himself also wrought the beginning; and it is He who does
> Himself say to Moses, "I have surely seen the affliction of
> my people which is in Egypt, and I have come down to de-
> liver them;" it being customary from the beginning with

the Word of God to ascend and descend for the purpose of saving those who were in affliction. (*Against Heresies* 4.12.4; ANF 1:476)

Early Christian typological interpretation of the exodus is not limited to the greatest events in that narrative. Indeed, it is often applied to some of its lesser details. This is seen in the comments of Caesarius of Arles on the rod of Moses:

That staff, dearly beloved, prefigured the mystery of the cross. Just as through the staff Egypt was struck by ten plagues, so also the whole world was humiliated and conquered by the cross. Just as Pharaoh and his people were afflicted by the power of the staff, with the result that he released the Jewish people to serve God, so the devil and his angels are wearied and oppressed by the mystery of the cross to such an extent that they cannot recall the Christian people from God's service. (*Sermons* 95.5; FC 47:67-68)

Similarly, Tertullian interprets the hand of Moses in the same chapter (Exod. 4) as a sign of the resurrection:

But we know that prophecy expressed itself by things no less than by words. By words, and also by deeds, is the resurrection foretold. When Moses puts his hand into his bosom, and then draws it out again dead, and again puts his hand into his bosom, and plucks it out living, does not this apply as a presage to all mankind? (*On the Resurrection of the Flesh* 28; ANF 3:565)

Moving further along in the narrative in Exodus, both Tertullian and Caesarius interpret the bitterness of the waters in Marah typologically:

Again, *water* is restored from its defect of "bitterness" to its native grace of "sweetness" by the tree of Moses. That tree was Christ, restoring, to wit, of Himself, the *veins* of some-time envenomed and bitter nature into the all-salutary *waters* of baptism. (Tertullian, *On Baptism* 9; ANF 3:673)

When the divine lesson was read yesterday, dearly beloved, we heard that after the crossing of the Red Sea the children of Israel came to Mara, that is, to bitter water. The people could not drink the water because it was bitter, and, there-fore, the Lord showed blessed Moses a tree which he cast into the water and it became sweet. Certainly, it is strange that He showed Moses a tree which he threw into the water to make it sweet. Just as if God could not have made the water sweet without the tree, or Moses did not know the tree, with the result that God showed it to him. Now we must see what the inner sense possesses in these matters that is suitable. The Red Sea signified the sacrament of Baptism; the bitter water designated the letter of the law. (Caesarius, *Sermons* 102.1-2; FC 47:103-4)

Similar quotations—hundreds of them—could easily be found. What is important in all this is not the interpretation of particular passages or events, but rather that when early Christians read the history of the deliverance of Israel from Egypt and the ensuing years in the desert, they saw in all of it—in its details as well as in its general drift—signs pointing to the saving work of Jesus.

Among ancient Christians the significance of Passover and the exodus was not limited to the field of biblical interpretation but also included the worship of the church. Passover, commem-orating the flight from Egypt, had a central place in the wor-ship traditions of Israel. It was the great celebration in which the people of Israel, in a meal that included, among other things, a lamb, remembered and reenacted the day when the blood of the lamb, marking the doors of their homes, saved each of their firstborns from the death that felled Egypt's firstborns and made it possible for the Israelites to finally leave Egypt. This was the reason for the Passover meal, whose purpose was not only to celebrate those events but also to make sure that future generations of Israelites were firmly grafted into the history of their people and what God had done for them.

For Christians, the typology of the exodus meant that their own worship was a way to become part of a new people that, like ancient Israel thanks to the paschal lamb, had been wrested from a condition of enslavement to sin and death thanks to the Lamb who takes away the sins of the world. When Paul declares that Christ is our Passover, he is expressing all of this in a concise and powerful way. What Christians do when they gather on the first day of the week—the day of the resurrection of the Lamb—to partake of a meal that is in many ways reminiscent of Israel's ancient traditions is to claim for themselves the history and identity of the people of God, jointly with the victory over the slavery of sin and death, a victory that is not their work but the Lamb's. This is why to this day many churches, when celebrating Communion, pray, "Lamb of God, who takes away the sins of the world, have mercy on us"—words that connect the long-standing Jewish celebration of Passover with the words of John the Baptist pointing to Jesus as the Lamb who, like the ancient lamb of the first Passover, died to save the people. Certainly, the celebration of the Lord's Supper is closely tied to the history of the exodus and the typology derived from it.

Likewise, because the crossing of the Red Sea was an act of liberation, and the crossing of the river Jordan was the entrance into the promised land, baptisms were traditionally performed on Easter Sunday, which commemorates the day when Jesus opened the gates of hell as he returned from death to life. Just as the bread of Communion was frequently related with the manna in the desert, the water of baptism was related with the waters of the Red Sea through which the people attained their new freedom, and the waters of the Jordan through which they came to their promised destination.

All of this means that the theology and the worship of the ancient church cannot be properly understood without taking into account the pivotal role of its typological connection to the exodus.

CHAPTER 15

Crucial Texts: The Word

The Gospel of John presents Jesus as the incarnate Word of God. The Greek word that most of our Bibles translate as "Word" is *Logos*. The term *Logos* is difficult to translate, for it has several meanings, all of them intertwined and each nuancing the rest. In brief, *Logos* means "word," "reason," "speech," "order." In ancient times, Greek-speaking philosophers used the various nuances of this word to express the connection among such concepts as mind, order, justice, and wisdom. Therefore, it was not uncommon for philosophers to speak of the Logos.

Given the philosophical use of the term *Logos*, its repeated use in the first verses of the Gospel of John has led many to the conclusion that the Fourth Gospel is an attempt to present the life and message of Jesus making use of the surrounding philosophical climate, thus making it more appealing to gentiles. This is the main reason why one often hears that this particular Gospel is "more philosophical" or "more Greek" that the others. But biblical scholars have pointed out that much of what is said in that Gospel about the Logos is similar to what is found in ancient Hebrew literature regarding Wisdom. If we read, for instance, Proverbs 8, we will see that much of what Proverbs says about Wisdom is what John also says about the Logos—although Proverbs does not say Wisdom became flesh, as John says of the Logos (John 1:14). Therefore, it is quite likely that the first verses of this Gospel—what is often called the "prologue" of John—are in fact a hymn inspired much more by Hebrew tradition that by Hellenism.

However, there is no doubt that from an early date there were Christians who began interpreting what the Fourth Gospel says about the Word in terms of the philosophical thought of the time, and that this resulted in the doctrine of the Logos becoming a sort of bridge between biblical tradition and Greco-Roman culture.

In classical Greek philosophy, the notion of the Logos served to explain why there is order in the universe and why that order corresponds with the order in our minds. The order of the world, by which all complex movements of the heavenly bodies are ruled, is the work of the Logos. There is no necessity for the heavenly bodies to move as they do, were their courses not set by the Logos, by the ordering principle of all things. Furthermore, this order is also imprinted in our minds. If our mind tells us that two plus two is four, we expect that when we check this out with realities outside our minds, it will prove to be true. And we find this to be the case. Two stones and two more stones are four stones; two apples and two more apples are four apples; and so forth in any case we may encounter in the entire world. We are so used to this that we are not puzzled by it. But if we take time to reflect on it, we realize first of all that the very existence of order in the world needs to be explained, and second, that the correspondence between that order and the thought processes of our minds also needs to be explained. It was at this point that Greek philosophers had recourse to the theory or doctrine of the Logos. The Logos is the reason or order underlying all reality, mental as well as physical. It is because of this underlying order that what reason tells us—for instance, that two and two are four—turns out to be true of the world outside our minds. This is why even today we say that something is "logical"—that is, that it has Logos. If something is illogical, if it makes no sense, it is because is runs counter to the order underlying all reality.

By the first century, philosophers had carried this notion of the Logos a bit further. Logos is not only the order undergirding the entire universe. It is also an active force that makes its way into the human mind in order to give it knowledge. We know not just because we observe but because the Logos teaches us. Thus, the Logos is both an underlying order and a power that leads the mind in the direction of that order.

Given all of this, ancient Christians, joining this philosophical tradition regarding the Logos with the opening words of the Gospel of John, soon came to claim that the one who took on flesh in Jesus Christ is none other than the very order that organizes all of creation and makes it reasonable, dependable, and *logical*. This view played an important role for Christian theologians in the second century, when people, hearing about Christianity, commented about it. The commonly held opinion among the masses was that Christianity was a sort of madness, a fanaticism typical of the uncultured. Some Christians who were committed to showing the untruth of such opinions—primarily those who are today called the "Greek apologists"—made use of philosophical views regarding the Logos in their arguments defending their faith. Since Proverbs 8 and other Hebrew wisdom literature affirm that Wisdom is the very order that the Creator employed in the creation of all things, in appropriating Greek notions about the Logos these apologists were not drifting far away from biblical tradition.

The outstanding figure among these Christian authors was Justin Martyr. Since the Gospel of John says not only that all things were made by the Logos but also that this Logos is "the true light, which enlightens everyone," one may affirm that wherever there is true light or true knowledge, that light and that knowledge come from the same Word or Logos of God whom we know thanks to the incarnation. Justin says:

> We have been taught that Christ is the first-born of God, and we have declared above that He is the Word of whom every race of men were partakers; and those who lived reasonably are Christians, even though they have been thought atheists; as, among the Greeks, Socrates and Heraclitus, and men like them; and among the barbarians, Abraham, and Ananias, and Azarias, and Misael, and Elias, and many others whose actions and names we now decline to recount, because we know it would be tedious. So that even they who lived before Christ, and lived without reason, were wicked and hostile to Christ, and slew those who lived reasonably. But who, through the power of the Word, according to the will of God the Father and Lord of all, He was born of a virgin as a man, and was named Jesus, and was crucified, and died, and rose again, and ascended into heaven, an intelligent man will be able to comprehend from what has been already so largely said. (*First Apology* 46; ANF 1:178)

This allowed Christians to claim the best of Greco-Roman philosophy as part of their own legacy, bequeathed to them by the Logos who was incarnate in Jesus. Having made that claim on philosophy, they could also seek to ground their understanding of their faith on it. This view evolved to the point that late in that second century, just a few decades after Justin, Clement of Alexandria would affirm that there are two covenants or paths leading to Jesus Christ. One of these is the covenant of the law, given to Israel. The other is the covenant of philosophy, given to the Greeks. From that point on, with notable exceptions, most

Christian theologians have followed a similar path in the task of building bridges between their faith and their culture.

The most common understanding of these matters follows the line of Augustine, who affirms the relationship between the prologue to the Gospel of John and Greek philosophy while also affirming that there is a uniquely Christian note in the doctrine of incarnation and redemption through Jesus Christ.

> And therein [in the books of Platonist philosophers] I read, not indeed in the same words, but to the selfsame effect, enforced by many and divers reasons, that, "In the beginning was the Word, and the Word was with God, and the Word was God. The same was in the beginning with God. All things were made by Him; and without Him was not any thing made that was made." That which was made by Him is "life; and the life was the light of men. And the light shineth in darkness; and the darkness comprehendeth it not." And that the soul of man, though it "bears witness of the light," yet itself "is not that light; but the Word of God, being God, is that true light that lighteth every man that cometh into the world." And that "He was in the world, and the world was made by Him, and the world knew Him not." But that "He came unto His own, and His own received Him not. But as many as received Him, to them gave He power to become the sons of God, even to them that believe on His name." This I did not read there. (*Confessions* 7.9.13; *NPNF*[1] 1:107-8)

In other words, Platonism seems to say the same as John's prologue, except that it does not know of the incarnation of the Logos in Jesus. For Augustine, as well as for much of Christian tradition, this is an enormous difference, since the incarnation of God in Christ is at the very foundation of Christian faith.

On this point one may add that, while Christians had resort to the doctrine of the Logos to relate their faith to Greek and other cultures, they have not always done so. Sadly, as one reviews the history of the expansion of Christianity, a general picture emerges in which the Logos theory was employed to build bridges only with the cultures of peoples that Christians could not overwhelm. A clear example is the missionary work of Matteo Ricci and his fellow Jesuits in China. Ricci sought to understand and to appreciate Chinese culture to such a point that Chinese intellectuals considered him a sage. But on the other hand, there is the case of the European conquest of the Americas, in which very little attention was given to the cultures already existing in these lands, as if the Logos had never been here, and as if it were only the Europeans who had any claim to the illumination of the Logos. Similarly, sub-Saharan Africa was said to be a land of ignorance, and the task of bringing "culture" to the continent often served as a justification for colonialism and even slavery.

There was another context in which the Logos tradition had an important role in Christian theology: the debates and often acrimonious controversies surrounding the Trinity. According to the Fourth Gospel, the Logos of God is not only the source of all light or knowledge. The Logos is actually divine. In the dominant forms of Platonism in the early centuries of the Christian era, the Logos was an intermediate being between the supreme Idea of goodness and beauty, which is absolutely immutable, and the mutable world of existing realities. According to some texts in Plato's dialogues, but even more so in later Platonism, there has to be an intermediate being between the immutable and the mutable, between the ineffable and unchanging Supreme Being and this world characterized by change and instability. This intermediate being, often called the demiurge, drawing inspiration from the beauty of the Supreme Being, becomes the creative agent of all that exists in the world. Since many Christian thinkers and writers soon adopted the notion of an immutable God or Supreme Being after the fashion of the Platonists, they had to face the difficulty of explaining how the immutable could relate with the mutable—how God could relate with the world. Some responded to this challenge by claiming that the Logos to which the Fourth Gospel refers is an intermediary, a sort of bridge—a demiurge—between the immutable God and the mutable creation. This would mean that the one relating directly with the world is not the immutable God, but rather the Word or Logos of God. According to this view, it is not the Father who acts and is revealed in the history of Israel and in the Scriptures. Nor is God the Father, the Supreme Being, the one who intervenes in history. Instead it is the Word of God, the Logos, who acts in the world, intervenes in history, and is revealed to humankind. In a word, the Logos or Word of God became a sort of go-between, not quite divine and yet above all creation.

The problem with such a view was that it required that the Word, Logos, or Son of God be inferior to the immutable Father. From the very beginning, Christians had worshiped the Son of God. But now some were claiming that the Son is not as truly divine as the Father. These views were held and defended by, among others, a presbyter in Alexandria whose name was Arius. They were absolutely rejected by Alexander, the bishop of Alexandria, as well as by most other Christian leaders.

The essential point is that, because of the Platonic influences mentioned above, there was a general agreement that made the Son of God an intermediary being between the Father and the world. If one then asks where the line is to be drawn between Creator and creation, the Arians would declare that the Son is part of creation, whereas Alexander and the Council of Nicaea would insist on the full divinity of the Son.

The ensuing controversies were bitter, and did not end soon, for the Council of Nicaea, which in 325 took a stand against Arianism, did not put an end to them. Although this is not the place to even outline the course of the debates and their political entanglements, it is important to realize that Constantine's successor, Constantius, favored and promoted Arianism. In 381 a second council, gathering in Constantinople, reiterated and developed what had been determined in Nicaea.

The result of these controversies is still reflected in Christian worship in various ways. The Gloria Patri, often sung as a doxology in many churches, is an affirmation of the equal divinity of Father, Son, and Holy Spirit, for it declares that divine glory is due to all three, "as it was in the beginning, is now, and ever shall be."

The same is affirmed in the Nicene Creed, often repeated in many churches—although what goes by that name is not exactly the creed affirmed at Nicaea, but includes later additions that were mostly added in and around the Council of Constantinople in 381, and therefore should more properly be called the Niceno-Constantinopolitan Creed. In this creed there are several declarations that clearly address what was seen as the Arian menace: "eternally begotten of the Father before all worlds, God of God, Light of Light, very God of very God, begotten, not made, being of one substance with the Father . . ."

Leaving aside the subtleties of that debate, one can clearly affirm, with the Gospel of John, that as Christians, we believe that our Lord Jesus the Christ is that Word, that Logos, that was present when God said, "Let there be . . . ," who was there when John the Baptist called him "the Lamb of God who takes away the sin of the world," who is present today as we call on him, and who will be there welcoming us to a great nuptial feast at the end of time.

CHAPTER 16

Lessons from the Past and Promises for the Future

A s one reviews the entire history of the Bible in the ancient church and the long process whereby that ancient Bible has come to us through the centuries, there are both lessons to be learned from the past and promises for the future. Furthermore, if one ponders the lessons from the past, they are soon transmuted into promises—or at least suggestions or glimpses—of the future. Drastically reducing what could be a vast theological treatise, one may say that these lessons/promises are essentially three.

The first lesson is that the Bible would not have reached us were it not for the labors of generation after generation who bequeathed it to us. When Paul wrote to the Galatians, he added to his epistle, obviously transcribed by a scribe, a personal note: "See what large letters I make when I am writing in my own hand!" (Gal. 6:11). Yet in our Bibles, no matter what version they may be, we find that the letters in Galatians 6:11 are exactly the same size as the rest of the text. Even when the very first copy of the epistle was made, the difference in the letters would have already disappeared. In other words, not only do we not have the autograph text of the epistle (or of any other book in the Bible), but what we have is the result of the interest and commitment of those first copyists who felt that what Paul was saying should be more widely shared. Therefore, the first lesson to be learned and remembered is that the Bible is best preserved not by storing it with great care, as the treasure it is, but by sharing it generously, precisely because it is a great treasure that all should possess. This lesson is then both a challenge and a promise. The challenge is to continue the work of transmitting and teaching Scripture as a grateful tribute to those generations who did likewise for us. We have no way of knowing how many generations will come after us before the end of all time. But we do know that each and every one of those generations will need to hear and heed the word of God. And this too is a promise: just as the work of the many who spent long hours and long years copying a Bible has borne fruit in us, so will our endeavors today to continue passing it on bear fruit in the morrow.

A second lesson to be learned from the entire process is that the Bible has come to us through innumerable copyists, translators, and interpreters, none of whom was infallible. As we now look at them and their understanding of the faith, we find them wanting in many respects. This should serve as a warning to us, that having the word of God at hand does not make us infallible. We too are falling into error, just as those copyists, translators, and interpreters did. Therefore, as we study Scripture and claim to base our doctrines, lives, and actions on it, we must do so with the humility of mortal sinners.

Finally, the physical changes in the Bible that we followed in the early chapters of this book should remind us that the Bible is the word of God not because of its format or appearance but because God speaks to us in it. The most ancient Bibles we have were themselves a sort of innovation. As we learned, the ancient Hebrew Bibles were scrolls, mostly leather. When Christianity began spreading, two significant changes soon occurred: instead of leather, Bibles were now reproduced in either papyrus or parchment; and instead of scrolls, they were now codices. We may well imagine some ancient believer complaining, "The Bible is not what it used to be. I grew up with leather scrolls. And now they are writing it on papyrus codices! People should show more respect for the Bible!" Much later, paper came to take the place of both parchment and papyrus. Perhaps then, once again, someone would have complained, "Those cheap Bibles are a scandal! The word of God deserves the best material!" As we have seen, when the movable-type printing press entered the scene, there were those who complained that the Bible should be kept in manuscript form, for copying it was a spiritual exercise that should not be lost. Each of these changes brought suspicion and criticism. Yet, as we now look back at them, we see that God was making sure the Bible would reach this twenty-first century of the Christian era.

Today, in our century, the Bible is once again taking shapes that would have seemed impossible a few decades ago. Many believers no longer carry the Bible under their arms, as I did in some of my earliest memories. Today we carry it on a phone, or on a tablet, or perhaps even in a watch! That lady two seats over on the subway wearing earphones may be listening to the prophet Isaiah—the same prophet whom the Ethiopian traveler was reading. Today there are electronic aids to Bible study that allow us to do in a few minutes research that would otherwise take years. And today also, as in the past, we have people (sometimes I find myself among them!) who say, "What has happened to those beautiful large, leather-bound Bibles we used to have on our coffee tables? Or those others, much smaller but still beautifully printed, that we carried to church or to Sunday school? I feel strange when the pastor, visiting me in the hospital, pulls out a phone to read a psalm!" And yet, if the entire history we have so rapidly reviewed tells us something, it is first of all that the shape of the Bible has been undergoing numerous changes through the centuries; and that, through all those transformations, it is still the same Bible, with the same power to transform us, to transform the church, and to transform society.

Therefore, this lesson from the past is also a promise for the future: be it in scrolls or codices, on parchment or paper, in printed or digital format, the word of God is still the same. And the promise is the same: this word that God sends out will not return to God empty but will accomplish that for which it was sent!

Cast of Characters

The brevity of this survey may have left you desiring to know more about some of the people and documents mentioned. What follows is a brief explanation of each. For further information, you may wish to look at other literature by or about the listed author; the sources of some of these other materials are abbreviated as follows:

HCT   *A History of Christian Thought*, rev. ed. 3 vols. Nashville: Abingdon, 1970.

HECL   *A History of Early Christian Literature*. Louisville: Westminster / John Knox, 2019.

TSC   *The Story of Christianity*, rev. ed. 2 vols. New York: Harper Collins, 2010.

Ambrose of Milan (ca. 339–397). Bishop of that city. Famous preacher who was instrumental in Augustine's conversion. Most of his writings are biblical commentaries and sermons, as well as translations from Greek into Latin. His two best known writings are *On the Mysteries* and *On the Duties of the Clergy*. HECL 243–55; TSC 1:219–24.

Apostolic Constitutions. A document of unknown date, probably from the late fourth century but reflecting earlier conditions. It deals mostly with the practical life and order of the church.

Aquinas, Thomas. *See* Thomas Aquinas

Athanasius (ca. 300-373). Bishop of Alexandria and champion of the Nicene faith. His theology revolves around the doctrine of incarnation. Among his main works are *On the Incarnation of the Word of God* and the *Life of Anthony*. HCT 1:291-302; HECL 186-198; TSC 1:199-208.

Augustine of Hippo (324-430). Commonly known as Saint Augustine. Possibly the most important theologian of Western Christianity. Hundreds of his writings are extant. The most influential among them are his *Confessions* and *The City of God*. HCT 2:15-55; HECL 292-312; TSC 1:241-52.

Basil the Great (329-379). Bishop of Caesarea in Cappadocia. Defender of Nicene theology in the generation following Athanasius. His main theological works are *Against Eunomius, On the Holy Spirit,* and *On the Six Days of Creation* (or *On the Hexameron*). But most engaging are his homilies, many of them on social issues. HCT 1:303-11; HECL 219-24; TSC 1:211-13.

Barnabas, Epistle of. A pseudonymous writing that seems to be a homily rather than an epistle. Possibly written in Alexandria ca. 150. Part of the Apostolic Fathers corpus. HCT 1:83-86; HECL 21-22.

Benedict of Nursia (ca. 480-543). Commonly known as Saint Benedict. Author of the Benedictine Rule, for centuries the most common monastic rule in the Western church. HECL 376-81; TSC 1:277-81.

Caesarius of Arles (470-542). A famous preacher who staunchly resisted the Pelagian tendencies of his times. His main work is *On Grace and Free Will.*

Calvin, John (1509-1564). The main theologian and one of the founders of the Reformed tradition. Born in France, he became the leader of the Reformation in Geneva, from where his influence soon reached as far as Scotland in one direction and Constantinople in the other—and eventually throughout the world. His main work is *Institutes of the Christian Religion.* HCT 3:133-77; TSC 2:77-86.

Cassiodorus (490-ca. 585). Full name: Flavius Magnus Aurelius Cassiodorus. Lived in Italy under the Ostrogoth regime and founded an influential monastery at Vivarium. His main work is *Institutes of Divine and Secular Letters.* HCT 2:69-71.

Cisneros, Francisco Jiménez (Ximenes) de (1436-1517). Spanish cardinal, and regent of the kingdom. A scholar who founded the University of Alcalá de Henares and promoted the scholarly work leading to the Complutensian Polyglot Bible. HCT 3:197-98; TSC 2:136-38.

Clement of Alexandria (died ca. 213). One of the first teachers and scholars—and in a way the founder—of the school of Alexandria. He employed the philosophical notion of the Logos to build apologetic bridges between the Christian faith and Greek philosophy, claiming that such philosophy was given by God to the Greeks with a purpose parallel to the giving of the law to Israel: to lead to Christ. HCT 1:186-204; HECL 88-96; TSC 1:86-88.

Clement of Rome (ca. 35-99). Bishop of that city. Under his leadership, the church in Rome sent a letter to the church in

Corinth. This letter, now called the First Epistle of Clement to the Corinthians, is counted among the writings of the Apostolic Fathers. (A Second Epistle to the Corinthians, attributed to him, is not his and is not really an epistle.) HCT 1:62–67; HECL 11–16; TSC 1:83.

Cyril of Jerusalem (313–386). Bishop of that city. His *Catechetical Lectures* is a valuable source for the study of the history of preparation for baptism, and of baptism itself. HECL 238–42.

Didache. A document of uncertain date, probably from the late first century, and apparently written in the desertic areas of Syria or in some other dry and arid region. Its first half is the "Document of the Two Ways," which is similar to a section of the Epistle of Barnabas. The second half includes instructions on baptism and Communion. It is counted among the Apostolic Fathers. HCT 1:67–71; HECL 9–11.

Diognetus, Address to. A document probably dating from the middle of the second century, and therefore perhaps the most ancient extant Christian apology. It is widely appreciated for its clear and inspiring style. Usually included among the Apostolic Fathers. HCT 1:116–17; HECL 29–31; TSC 1:62.

Egeria. A pilgrim from Galicia to the Holy Land, ca. 379. She has left a travel diary that she wrote as a report to her sisters in Galicia. The portion of her diary that is still extant is of enormous value for its descriptions of religious practices in the Greek-speaking East. HECL 269–71.

Ephrem Syrus (died ca. 373). A prolific writer in Syriac. He attended the Council of Nicaea and afterward spent most of his life in Edessa. Besides being a significant theologian, he was also a poet whose hymns are still sung today. HECL 278–79.

Erasmus (1466–1536). A famous Dutch scholar who was one of the main figures in sixteenth-century humanism. A Catholic seeking the reformation of the church, but not in the way Luther proposed. His most important contribution to biblical studies was his critical edition of the New Testament, published in 1516. HCT 3:21–28; TSC 2:14–18.

Eusebius of Caesarea (ca. 260–339). Often considered the father of church history. Making use of the library that Origen had gathered in Caesarea, he wrote his *Church History* as well as *Preparation for the Gospel* and *Demonstration of the Gospel*. He was an important figure in the Council of Nicaea. HECL 177–85; TSC 1:149–55.

Gregory the Great (ca. 540–604). Bishop of Rome from 590 to his death. He did much to restore order in western Europe after the Germanic invasions of the previous centuries and thus became a landmark in the growing power and prestige of the papacy. Besides numerous sermons, epistles, and other writings, he wrote a *Pastoral Rule* that became the textbook from which many medieval pastors learned how to deal with people in various circumstances or with varying attitudes. HCT 2:71–73; HECL 377–85; TSC 1:285–88.

Hermas (mid-second century). A brother of Pius, the bishop of Rome. His single writing, commonly known as the Shepherd of Hermas, is a compilation of visions, similitudes, and commandments that he seems to have preached in Rome. It is included among the Apostolic Fathers. HCT 1:86–90; HECL 22–26.

Hippolytus (ca. 175-235). A rigoristic and traditionalist theologian who led the opposition in Rome, first to Bishop Zephyrinus, and then to his successor Calixtus. Elected as a rival bishop of Rome, he therefore presents us with the anomaly of a person whom the Roman Catholic Church considers both an antipope and a saint. His main works are *Refutation of All Heresies* and *The Apostolic Tradition*. The latter is one of the most valuable extant sources for the history of early Christian worship. HCT 1:229-35; HECL 114-23.

Ignatius of Antioch (died 108). Bishop of Antioch sentenced to die as a martyr in Rome. On the way to the capital as a prisoner, he wrote seven letters that are one of the most precious jewels of ancient Christian literature. His letters are included among the Apostolic Fathers. HCT 1:71-80; HECL 16-20; TSC 51-53.

Irenaeus (ca. 130-202?). Bishop of Lyons. Originally from Smyrna, where he seems to have been a disciple of Polycarp. Author of two important works: *Against Heresies* and *Demonstration of Apostolic Preaching*. HCT 1:157-70; HECL 77-87; TSC 84-86.

Jerome (ca. 347-420). Biblical scholar best known for his translation of Scripture into Latin, known as the Vulgate. HECL 256-66; TSC 233-39.

Justin (middle of second century). A philosopher who traveled from his native Samaria in a quest for truth, and died as a martyr in Rome—therefore commonly known as "Justin Martyr." He wrote two apologies (defenses) of Christian faith and the *Dialogue with Trypho*, which deals with the relationship between Christianity and the Hebrew Scriptures. HCT 1:101-9; HECL 33-40; TSC 62-66.

Langton, Stephen (1150-1228). A professor of theology at the university of Paris, and then archbishop of Canterbury. He was among the leaders of the movement that resulted in the signing of the Magna Carta. TSC 1:366.

Lombard, Peter. *See* Peter Lombard

Luther, Martin (1483-1546). An Augustinian monk and professor at the University of Wittenberg, where the Protestant Reformation was born in 1517. Translator of the Bible into German. HCT 3:29-69; TSC 2:47-56.

Marcion (second century). The son of a bishop in Pontus. Expelled as a heretic from the church of Rome in 144. He proposed a radical discontinuity between the faith of Israel and that of the church. He therefore rejected the Hebrew Scriptures, which he considered the revelation of a lesser god. He proposed a canon of the New Testament that consisted of the Gospel of Luke and the Epistles of Paul, both purged of any reference to the Hebrew Scriptures. HCT 1:137-43; TSC 1:73-74.

Melanchthon, Philip (1497-1560). A professor at the University of Wittenberg, where he became Luther's chief support. Known particularly as the reformer of the German educational system. HCT 3:104-10.

Melito of Sardis (second century). Bishop of that city. All that remains of his work, besides a few fragments, is his *Paschal Sermon*. HCT 1:117-18; HECL 44.

Muratori, Ludovico Antonio (1672-1750). An Italian scholar known mostly for his biblical studies and his discovery of a brief text now bearing his name, the Muratorian Canon.

Origen (ca. 185-253). One of the most famous Christian scholars of antiquity. He was born and raised in Alexandria but later moved to Caesarea due to conflicts with the bishop of Alexandria. His literary production is astonishing. Much of this is still extant, although much has also been lost. In the field of biblical studies, he produced the *Hexapla* Bible, with six columns comparing various texts and versions of Scripture, as well as numerous commentaries and homilies. HCT 1:205-27; HECL 124-34; TSC 1:93-96.

Papias of Hierapolis (second century). Bishop of that city who sought to collect data about the sayings of Jesus and about the apostles. All that remains of his extensive writings is a few fragments, dealing mostly with the origin of the Gospels and with the promised eschatological abundance. HCT 1:82-83; HECL 26-27; TSC 1:36.

Peter Lombard (1096-1160). A theologian who became bishop of Paris, and an important forerunner of scholasticism. Known mostly for his four books of *Sentences*, which became the main textbook for medieval scholasticism. HCT 2:178-81; TSC 1:372.

Pliny the Elder (ca. 23-79). A prolific pagan author whose *Natural History* is a veritable encyclopedia.

Pliny the Younger (61-ca. 113). Governor in Bithynia who in 112 wrote Emperor Trajan, reporting on the inquiries he had made into Christianity and requesting instructions on the policies to be followed regarding Christians. He was a nephew of Pliny the Elder. TSC 1:49-51.

Polycarp of Smyrna (second century). Bishop of that city to whom Ignatius of Antioch wrote one of his seven letters. Later Polycarp wrote to the Philippians asking for news about Ignatius. Polycarp also died a martyr. His trial and execution are told in the *Martyrdom of Polycarp*. He is counted among the apostolic fathers. HCT 1:80-82; HECL 20-21, 45-46; TSC 1:53-55.

Pseudo-Dionysius (late fifth century). An author deeply influenced by Platonism who claimed to be the Dionysius who was converted through Paul's ministry in Athens—Dionysius the Areopagite. He wrote, among other works, *The Celestial Hierarchy*, *The Ecclesiastical Hierarchy*, and *Mystical Theology*. Since he was believed to be a direct disciple of Paul, he enjoyed great authority in the Middle Ages. HCT 2:93-96; HECL 392-94; TSC 1:319.

Tatian (second century). A disciple of Justin, with whom he disagreed on the value of Greek philosophy. Besides the apology *Address to the Greeks*, he composed a compilation of the four Gospels into one, the *Diatessaron*. This was widely used in the Syrian churches for centuries. HCT 1:109-12; HECL 40-41; TSC 1:63-64.

Tertullian (ca. 160-ca. 240). Author of the first significant Christian literature in Latin. Thus, also the creator of much Christian Latin theological vocabulary. He wrote extensively against various heresies as well as on the practices of Christian life. He had a legalistic tendency that he bequeathed to later Western theology. HCT 1:171-85; HECL 97-106; TSC 1:88-93.

Thomas Aquinas (1225-1274). The most important of all medieval theologians. Commonly known as the "Angelic Doctor," he was a Dominican professor at the University of Paris.

Besides several commentaries on Scripture, on the *Sentences* of Peter Lombard, and on the works of Aristotle, he wrote *Summa contra Gentiles* and the monumental *Summa Theologiae*. His philosophical and theological system is known as "Thomism." HCT 2:261-81; TSC 1:375-80.

Valentinus (second century). One of the most influential gnostic teachers. He composed a Gospel of Truth that is still extant. HCT 1:134-37; HECL 59-60.

Further Reading

Bradshaw, Paul F. *Reconstructing Early Christian Worship*. London: SPCK, 2009.

Gamble, Harry Y. *Books and Reading in the Early Church*. New Haven, CT: Yale University Press, 1995.

Gamble, Harry Y. *The New Testament Canon: Its Making and Meaning*. Philadelphia: Fortress, 1985.

González, Justo L. *Christian Thought Revisited: Three Types of Theology*. Maryknoll, NY: Orbis, 1999.

González, Justo L. "How the Bible Has Been Interpreted in Christian Tradition." In *The New Interpreter's Bible*, vol. 1, 83-106. Nashville: Abingdon, 1994.

Grafton, Anthony. *Christianity and the Transformation of the Book*. Cambridge, MA: Harvard University Press, 1995.

Grant, Robert M. *The Formation of the New Testament*. New York: Harper & Row, 1965.

Haines-Eitzen, Kim. *Guardians of Letters: Literacy, Power, and the Transmitters of Early Christian Literature*. New York: Oxford University Press, 2000.

Harris, William V. *Ancient Literacy*. Cambridge, MA: Harvard University Press, 1989.

Hurtado, Larry W. *At the Origins of Christian Worship: The Context and Character of Earliest Christian Devotion*. Grand Rapids: Eerdmans, 2000.

King, Thomas F. *The Role of the Scroll*. New York: Norton, 2019.

Souter, Alexander. *The Text and Canon of the New Testament*. London: Duckworth, 1954.

Index of Names and Subjects

Index of Scripture References